MAMMALS
OF GREAT BRITAIN & EUROPE

Paul Morrison

"Investigator Series"

ASTON PUBLICATIONS

Published in 1992 by
Aston Publications Limited
Bourne End House, Harvest Hill,
Bourne End, Bucks, SL8 5JJ

ISBN 0 946627 71 1

Designed by Alan Oliver

Printed in Hong Kong

Sole distributors to the UK book trade
Springfield Books Limited
Norman Road, Denby Dale,
Huddersfield,
West Yorkshire, HD8 8TH

Paul Morrison, author, naturalist and wildlife photographer, has
spent many years watching mammals closely through binoculars and
camera lenses. Although a marine biologist by qualification, his
interest in wildlife is diverse and he has written books on subjects
ranging from butterflies to birds.

He has also travelled widely to photograph wildlife and has recently
returned from Antarctica and the Indian Ocean. He runs the wildlife
picture library Natural Selection and his book on the Falkland Islands
was published by Aston Publications in 1990.

Photograph Credits

All photographs supplied by **Natural Selection**. Individual credits
as follows:
Geoffrey Kinns, pages 8, 9, 10, 14, 16, 18, 19, 22, 23, 24, 25, 26, 27,
28, 29, 32, 34, 35, 38, 39, 40, 41, 42, 44, 45, 46, 47, 52, 55, 56, 57, 59,
64, 65, 66, 68, 69, 70, 72, 73, 74, 75, 76, 77, 78, 81, 82, 83, 84, 85, 86,
87, 88, 92, 93, 99, 106, 108, 110, 112, 118, 119, 122, 124, 125, 126,
127, 142, 143, 144, 145, 148, 149, 150, 151, 156, 157, 158. **W S Paton**,
pages 50, 80, 98, 100, 107, 111, 113, 116, 117, 123, 128, 129, 154,
155. **Paul Morrison**, pages 4, 5, 6, 7, 11, 71, 89, 96, 97, 132, 133,
134, 152, 153. **Claude Baranger**, pages 12, 13, 60, 62, 63, 137, 138,
140, 141. **Dr R E Stebbings**, pages 30, 31, 33, 36, 37, 43, 48, 49.
Andre Fatras, pages 67, 114, 115, 120, 121. **Michael Leach**, pages
15, 51, 90, 91, 101. **David Hosking**, pages 17, 20, 21. **Richard Revels**,
pages 79, 104, 159. **Wayne Towriss**, pages 146, 147. **Gordon
Langsbury**, pages 53, 105. **Eric Hosking**, page 61. **Richard Balharry**,
page 54. **A J Sutcliffe (Natural Science Photos)**, page 139. **Ken Cole
(Natural Science Photos)**, page 94. **Kennan Ward (Natural Science
Photos)**, page 130. **Brian Hawkes**, page 102. **Ian Beames**, page 103.
John W Warden (Natural Science Photos), page 131. **J F Young**,
page 109. **G Montalverne (Natural Science Photos)**, page 136.
E A Janes, page 58. **K Jayaram (Natural Science Photos)**, page 135.
L Lee Rue (Frank Lane Agency), page 95.

Cover Photographs:
Front: Red Deer and Calf (**Geoffrey Kinns**); Hazel Dormouse
(**Paul Morrison**)
Rear: Red Squirrel (**J F Young**); Fox Cub (**Paul Morrison**)

Contents

For Geoffrey Kinns – a naturalist who taught me so much.

Introduction

Mammals have been on this planet for nearly 200 million years. Today there are some 4500 known species in the world, of which 198 have been recorded in Europe. Only 100 of these have been seen in the British Isles where 50 are regarded as resident or indigenous species; the rest being introduced, feral (domestic animals living wild), or vagrant bats, whales, porpoises, dolphins and seals.

The British Isles has fewer mammals than neighbouring Europe. After the last Ice Age 10,000 years ago, Ireland and Wales were connected by land and England was connected with France and Holland. Mammals like the Mountain Hare, Stoat, Otter, Pine Marten and Red Fox all colonised Ireland by these land bridges. However, 5,000 years ago, as the sea levels rose, England was separated from continental Europe by the English Channel. Many species from southern Europe, failed to reach England before the sea cut them off. Mammals like the Garden Dormouse, Common Vole, Beech Marten and Pond Bat were thus prevented from colonising England.

Man has also been responsible for the dearth of mammals in Britain. The Lynx, Reindeer, Brown Bear and Wild Boar were all persecuted until they died out and the Beaver met with a similar fate in the 12th century. The Wolf was the final native British mammal to become extinct with the last Wolf killed in Scotland in 1743 and around 1770 in Ireland.

Ever since Neolithic man (3100–2900BC) began felling large areas of Britain's forest for cultivation and agriculture, man has unwittingly or deliberately altered the distribution and population of Britain's mammals. As habitats changed, certain species bred successfully and became more common. In the 11th century, during the Norman Invasion, trade between neighbouring countries increased and rabbits, rats, grey squirrels and several species of deer were introduced and have now become established in the wild.

Amongst many other characteristics, mammals are warm blooded (32–40°C/90–104°F), possess an internal, jointed skeleton, feed their young on milk and have hairy or furry bodies. Many are either nocturnal (active at night) or crepuscular (active at twilight) and together with their wary nature, are therefore difficult to see to all but the patient observer.

It is easier to watch mammals at certain times of the year. Winter is an ideal season because lack of vegetation provides a greater field of view and mammals are less able to hide. Rodent and carnivore burrows become more obvious and although some species hibernate, others like the Grey Squirrel periodically emerge to search for food. Midsummer is also an ideal time because the night-time is reduced and even the most nocturnal species like the Badger, begin their foraging in daylight.

Sight is not the keenest sense in many mammals, but sense of hearing and smell are well developed. The observers must therefore always position

Photographic hide made from local vegetation

themselves down wind and remain silent. For secretive mammals it i useful to construct a simple hide. Camouflaged fabric, stretched across portable framework is frequently used, but by building a rigid screen from local vegetation, it is possible to remain undetected (plate 1). The hide should be set up a few days before observations begin so that foraging mammals become acclimatised to it.

Some mammals respond to being fed regularly with bait and over a period of weeks they become conditioned to feed in the same place at a certain time. Close-up views and photographs of mammals such as Badgers, ca be obtained from a hide using this technique (plate 2). Much pleasure i obtained by watching Badgers, Red Fox, various deer and squirrel through binoculars. Those with 7x42 or 8x42 magnification are best because they have good light gathering powers, useful at twilight o dawnrise.

Naturalists should learn how to identify animal tracks and signs in the countryside, since these are often seen before the species. Droppings ar not necessarily deposited at random as many carnivores use them to mar their territories, depositing them on tufts of grass or a regularly use pathway. The most important characteristics to learn about mamma droppings are their size and overall appearance.

Footprints, like human fingerprints, possess unique features which mak

mammals like the Badger respond to bait

possible to identify a species of mammal or at least the Order. Correct identification of tracks is only possible when ground conditions are good and snow, bare soft mud and sand provide the clearest imprints. The drawings in this book outline the complete tracks with all their diagnostic features, but perfect tracks rarely occur in the field so they are best used as a guide to possible identification of a species. Tracks either show distinct hoof marks or "slots" created by the two central digits forming the hoof, or complete outlines with digits and claws. Some mammals like the Otter and Coypu have clear webs between the digits.

Tracks with clear digital outlines and claws also show prominent features such as digital (toe) pads, interdigital (palm or sole) pads and proximal heel) pads. These vary in size, shape and number and the tracks sometimes differ according to age and sex of the mammal. Track registration occurs whenever the hind-feet are placed in almost the same position as the fore-feet causing either total elimination or partial overprinting and a complicated mixture of the two tracks.

Groups of tracks form trails which themselves vary in appearance depending on whether the mammal was walking, running, bounding or hopping. The distance between the right and left tracks is called the straddle, whereas the distance between the tracks made by the same foot is the stride. During the walking gait when registration is often most clear, only one limb is lifted from the ground at a time and the stride is generally short. Such trails suggest the mammal has been leisurely feeding or foraging. By increasing pace, the mammal breaks into a run, when alternate opposite limbs are lifted off the ground at the same time e.g. left fore and right hind, and the stride increases. Those mammals with hooves show increased distortion in their tracks as their cleaves slip and splay in the mud. The running gait is typical of many insectivores, rodents and carnivores. Throughout this book the following abbreviations have been used: RF – right fore track; RH – right hind track; LF – left fore track and LH – left hind track.

Many deer, wild sheep and goats often move at a galloping pace when all four feet are off the ground together, at some instance during the stride. Smaller mammals like the weasel and rabbit bound or hop. In the bounding gait the entire body is lifted off the ground by the hind legs but the tracks occur in groups of four with the two hind and two fore tracks directly opposite each other. Sometimes the tracks are so closely grouped that partial registration occurs.

There are numerous other signs and clues left behind by mammals. Many mammals store their food in their burrows or in shallow caches. Others, like the Wood Mouse and Red Squirrel chew fir cones in a characteristic way so that positive identification is possible. Red Deer and Wild Boar enjoy wallowing in muddy pools whereas Moles, Badger and Red Fox excavate typical mounds or burrows which provide clues to their identification. Sometimes the smell of a Polecat or Red Fox lingers on vegetation or around the entrance to their dens and eventually becomes unmistakable, whereas the trained human ear will detect whistling Marmots or squeaking shrews amongst dense vegetation.

Watching mammals closely may lead to actively trying to protect certain species and their threatened habitats. In many countries of Europe individual animals are protected but their environments are not. In Europe each country has its own legislation to protect mammals. In Britain they are protected under the Wildlife and Countryside Act 1981, an Act of Parliament which represents the most comprehensive wildlife law. In 1986 following the first Quinquennial Review of the Act, the Pine Marten, Wild Cat, Hazel Dormouse and all species of whale, porpoise and dolphin were added to the already protected species.

The future of Britain's and Europe's mammals are in everybody's hands, not just professional mammalogists. Enthusiastic amateur naturalists have largely contributed to the overall knowledge of our mammals and have created awareness to aspects threatening their long-term survival. Only by continued interest and positive help will many species be protected and benefit from controlled reintroduction schemes.

In Great Britain, any reader interested in knowing more about mammals should contact **The Mammal Society, Dept of Zoology, University of Bristol, Woodland Road, Bristol BS8 1UG. Tel (0272) 272300.**

Red-necked Wallaby, found in Britain's Peak District

British Distribution

RED-NECKED WALLABY *Body length:* **60–70 cm** (24–27 in.) *Tail length:* **64cm** (25 in).

Macropus rufogriseus originated from the scrublands of Tasmania, but now roams parts of Britain, having escaped from wildlife parks during the last 130 years. The most famous colony live in the Peak District National Park, but only about 12 remain out of a population of 60 animals. They are the descendants of 5 wallabies that escaped in 1939, but harsh winters, disturbance by people and road and railway accidents have reduced their numbers. Other colonies occur in Ashdown Forest, Sussex, and sightings have been made around Loch Lomond. Regular sightings of individual wallabies occur in the Bedfordshire countryside and these are probably escapees from nearby Whipsnade Zoo. Elsewhere they have been seen around Burnham Beeches in south Buckinghamshire, but there is no confirmation of breeding colonies. Wallabies are shy, alert animals, hiding in woodlands, but also browsing on heather, grass and bracken in open country.

Not much larger than a Brown Hare, these wallabies have red-brown fur on their nape and shoulders with black tips to their long feet and tail. These features are easily seen when they bound away on their hind feet, tucking their forelimbs against their chests. A single youngster is born between March and May and spends up to 10 months in the pouch, after which it gradually becomes independent.

No European Distribution

European Distribution

Red-necked Wallaby (Order *Marsupialia*)

Similar species: Within its restricted British range, the Red-necked Wallaby cannot be mistaken for any other mammal.

Field signs and clues: The tracks are easily distinguished, especially in soft ground. The 5-digit foretrack measures 7 x 7cm (2.75 x 2.75in) and the claw marks are distinct, although the thumb print may be very insignificant or absent altogether. The hind tracks are large, measuring 12.5 x 5cm (5 x 2in), and comprise 3 digits. The central digit is well developed, whereas another is much smaller and the third is vestigial. Whenever the Wallaby rests, the full length of the foot up to the heel is revealed, making an imprint 25cm (10in) long.

Normally the Wallaby hops through the countryside on its hind legs so that only the hind tracks show, and with a stride ranging from 45–100cm (17.7–40in) depending on speed. If the animal has been walking slowly, then groups of four tracks will be found, with the paired hind tracks lying just in front of the smaller foretracks. This arrangement of prints occurs because, as the Wallaby takes a step, it swings its hind feet round the outside of the resting forefeet in a leap-frogging movement. The tail drag is also distinct in snow or soft mud, but only during the walking gait.

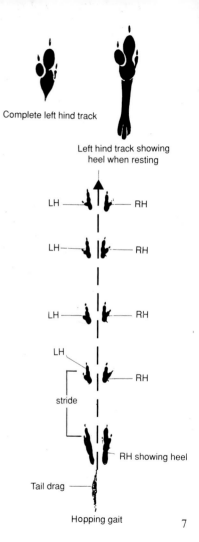

Complete left hind track

Left hind track showing heel when resting

LH — RH

LH — RH

LH — RH

LH

RH

stride

RH showing heel

Tail drag

Hopping gait

7

A family of young Hedgehogs

British Distribution

HEDGEHOG *Body length:* **20–30cm** (7.8–11.8 in).

The long, pointed snout and rounded body, covered with over 6000 spines, make *Erinaceus europaeus* unmistakable. The underside and most of the head are covered with dark brown or beige hairs, and the creamy-white spines, with a brown band near the tip, are themselves really modified hairs.

Found throughout Britain, apart from some of the northern islands, the Hedgehog inhabits woodland margins, hedgerows and scrubland, but is also commonly seen in suburban gardens and on golf courses. Although territories may overlap, hedgehogs are typically solitary animals and virtually nocturnal, when they forage for insects, worms, slugs and spiders, using their keen sense of smell. They are extremely agile, running, climbing and even swimming effectively. Their most familiar habit is rolling into a spiky ball when danger approaches, deterring all predators except the fox and badger. This natural reaction is no protection against the motor car and many thousands are killed annually on the roads.

After an elaborate courtship, beginning in April, 4 or 5 young are born in breeding nests made of dry leaves and grass between June and September. They leave the nest after 3 weeks, during which time they remain with the female (sow) and are still being suckled. The young become independent around October, when hibernation begins.

8

European Distribution

Hedgehog (Order *Insectivora*)

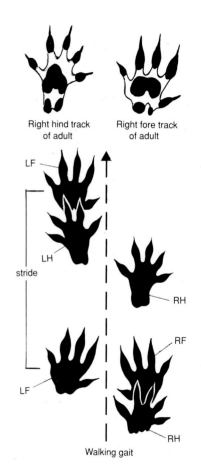

Right hind track of adult

Right fore track of adult

LF
LH
stride
LF

RH
RF
RH

Walking gait

Similar species: In Europe, the Algerian Hedgehog (*Erinaceus algirus*) and Eastern Hedgehog (*E.e. concolor*) are very similar, but in Britain the animal cannot be mistaken for any other species.
Field signs and clues: Both feet are approximately the same size with the forefeet measuring 4 x 2cm (1.57 x 1in) and the hind feet 4.5 x 2.5cm (1.77 x 1in). The digital marks are short and well separated from the large pads, whereas the sharp claw imprints are long. Both fore and hind feet have 5 digits. Hedgehogs normally move with a shuffling walk and the feet are turned slightly outwards, producing a stride of about 10cm (4in). The body rests close to the ground and the spines may drag in the mud, leaving characteristic marks. Whenever disturbed, hedgehogs hold their body well off the ground and run so that no spine drag occurs and the stride increases to 15–20cm (6–8in).

Apart from a few muffled snorts and snuffling sounds, hedgehogs are mostly silent, but during their courtship behaviour, loud snorts and grunts are uttered by both sexes. Hedgehog droppings are highly characteristic, being cylindrical and glossy black. They measure 2–4cm (0.78–1.6in) long and 1cm (0.4in) diameter and are randomly distributed as the hedgehog walks – especially across lawns.

Hedgehog dropping

9

Detail of Mole's head

British Distribution

MOLE *Body length:* **11–15cm** (4.3–6in).

Despite being rarely seen, the torpedo-shaped body and huge shovel-like forelimbs of *Talpa europaea* are well known. Occasionally the tapering head, with its sensory, pink, fleshy snout, is glimpsed above ground at a molehill, but these shy, elusive animals are perfectly adapted for subterranean life. Apart from the snout, mouth and feet, the body is covered in dense, velvety-black fur which conceals the ears and poorly functional eyes. The fur lies in either direction so that the Mole can rapidly reverse along its tunnels.

Except for Ireland and some of the Western Isles, the Mole is common throughout Britain and western Europe, inhabiting woodland, grassland, arable fields and gardens wherever the soil provides suitable tunnelling and a varied supply of invertebrate food.

Moles tunnel throughout the year, with the loose earth pushed up a vertical shaft and forming the characteristic molehills. From February to June, a grass-lined nest is formed in a deep tunnel. Generally 4 pink, naked young are suckled for the first month, after which body fur grows, and they leave the nest at 5 weeks. They are fully grown at 9 weeks and breed the following year.

European Distribution

Mole (Order *Insectivora*)

Similar species: In Europe, wherever their ranges overlap, both the Blind Mole (*Talpa caeca*) and the Roman Mole (*T. romana*) are similar, but in Britain the species is unmistakable.

Field signs and clues: Because of their underground lifestyles mole tracks are rarely seen. There are 5 digits on both fore and hind feet, but the front limbs are modified so that the Mole walks on the side of its feet, forming an L-shaped impression with claw marks, although all 5 don't always register in the track. Tracks are minute, about 1.5 x 1cm (0.6 x 0.4in) with a stride of 3–4 cm (1.18–1.57in). All surface tracks are extensively scuffed by the underside of the mole's body, which is always dragged across the ground. The surest sign of the presence of moles is a conical molehill on the soil surface, with a base diameter of around 30cm (12in). A row of molehills suggests deep underground tunnelling, whereas continuous surface ridges of earth indicate shallow tunnels.

Complete left hind track

Left hind track in hard ground

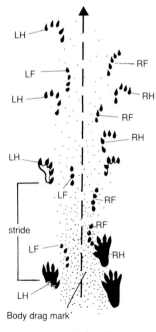

LH

LF

RF

LH

RH

RF

RH

LH

LF

RF

stride

RF

LF

RH

LH

Body drag mark

Walking gait

Pyrenean Desman eating an earthworm

No British Distribution

British Distribution

PYRENEAN DESMAN *Body length:* **11–13.5cm** (4.3–5.3in). *Tail length:* **13–15.5cm** (5.1–6.1in).

The solitary Pyrenean Desman (*Galemys pyrenaicus*) is so secretive that it was not discovered until 1811, when it became the last new mammal to be found in France. It is similar in appearance to a shrew, but with the rotundity of a mole, and its long, red, spatulate snout is its diagnostic feature. Totally confined to the clear mountain streams and lakes of the French and Spanish Pyrenees, this species seeks protection in rock crevices or holes beneath overhanging tree roots. Since it is nocturnal and hunts beneath the surface, the Desman is rarely seen. It rapidly zig zags through the water catching snails, crayfish and worms, rising to the surface only to gulp for air by poking its snout above the water like a snorkel. Its sensitive nose is the Desman's major contact with the surrounding world, since the animal is virtually blind. The nose is used to probe every crevice for food and as a digging tool in the mud at the bottom of streams. Mating occurs during January–February and 2–5 young are born between March and July and suckled for 4 weeks. They become independent soon afterwards and reach sexual maturity the following year.

European Distribution

Pyrenean Desman (Order *Insectivora*)

Typical silhouette of Pyrenean Desman seen at night when perched on rocks.

Similar species: Although much larger, the Pyrenean Desman is sometimes confused with the Water Shrew (*Neomys fodiens*, page 18).

Field signs and clues: This is one of Europe's most difficult mammals to observe because of its restricted range, aquatic lifestyle and nocturnal activity. One of the few signs is a constant stream of bubbles emitted from the muzzle during feeding under water. These rise to the surface in a moving silvery stream, but similar bubbles are also caused by a feeding Water Shrew. Occasionally their small, black, twisted droppings are found, deposited on large stones protruding above the water. This is the most positive sign that a stretch of river is colonized, and the territories extend for about 182m (597ft).

The tracks rarely show up, but are sometimes located in the soft mud at the river margins, where the water is shallow. Both fore and hind feet have 5 digits with sharp claws and the tracks are similar to those of the Water Shrew but with additional web markings on the hind feet.

Detail of Common Shrew's head

British Distribution

COMMON SHREW *Body length:* **5.4–8.5cm** (2.13–3.35in). *Tail length:* **3.2–5.6cm** (1.26–2.2in).

    One of Britain's most common mammals, *Sorex araneus* is rarely seen because it conceals itself in dense vegetation. Its tri-coloured coat is distinctive, with dark brown back, pale underside and light brown flanks. The colour of the back varies according to age, being paler in juveniles. With long, pointed nose, small, rounded ears and tiny eyes, the Common Shrew is easily distinguished from mice or voles.

    Activity is continuous throughout the day, all year round, with the shrew rushing through the undergrowth searching for invertebrates, especially earthworms, woodlice and spiders. Like the Pygmy Shrew, food has to be found every few hours if it is to survive. The Common Shrew is found in all habitats with ground cover, although it is scarce on moorland and only colonizes mountainsides up to the summer snowline. Absent from Ireland and some offshore islands the Common Shrew is found throughout the rest of the British Isles and Europe, except the Iberian Peninsula and Iceland. Several litters of 6–8 young are born from April onwards.

European Distribution

14

Common Shrew (Order *Insectivora*)

Similar species: The Common Shrew is similar to the Pygmy Shrew (*Sorex minutus*, page 16, the Greater White-toothed Shrew (*Crocidura russula*, page 20) and the Lesser White-toothed Shrew (*Crocidura Suaveolens*, page 22).

Field signs and clues: It is rare to find tracks in the wild except in dry, fine silt. They are minute, the forefeet measuring 8 x 9mm (0.3 x 0.35in) and the hind feet 1 x 1cm (0.39 x 0.39in), and all tracks have 5 digits with distinct pads and sharp claws. Usually the Common Shrew moves with a running gait with a stride of 4cm (1.57in), but in the bounding gait the 4 tracks are grouped together with about 5cm (1.96in) between each group. A tail-drag is always clearly visible once a trail is discovered.

It is often a high-pitched squeaking from dense grass or dry undergrowth that is the first sign of shrews being present, but the discovery of corpses is also a frequent observation. Shrews die of old age at the end of their second summer and can be found in large numbers.

The shrew's tunnels and nests can be found in dry, surface vegetation and beneath fallen trees. The nests are flimsy, woven balls of grass, usually built in dense vegetation on the surface of the soil, and the network of tunnels is horizontally flattened in cross section and often continues beneath discarded metal sheets or planks of wood.

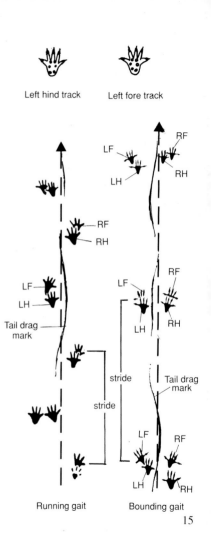

Left hind track   Left fore track

LF
LH
RF
RH

RF
RH

LF
LH

Tail drag mark

stride

stride

Running gait

RF
RH

LF
LH

LF
LH

RF
RH

Tail drag mark

LF
LH

RF
RH

Bounding gait

15

Pygmy Shrew foraging

British Distribution

PYGMY SHREW *Body length:* **4–6cm** (1.5–2.3in). *Tail length:* **4.5–6.5cm** (1.77–2.5in).

Sorex minutus, as its name suggests, is Britain's smallest mammal. The fur is brown with paler underparts and the nose is typically pointed, extending from a bulbous head. Despite their size, Pygmy Shrews are very hardy, colonizing every habitat from sea level to mountain top, where they constantly forage for prey and only stop moving for a few minutes each day. The shrew has such a high metabolism that it would starve if it was unable to find food within two hours. Prey includes spiders, insects and their larvae.

Although they are found throughout the British Isles and most of Europe, except the Iberian Peninsula, they are rarer than the Common Shrew, with which they share both habitats and range. Breeding occurs April–August, with 4–7 young born in a nest often below ground or concealed in a grass tussock. Several litters are produced each year and the young leave their nests after about 3 weeks. Early-born youngsters are able to breed before the end of the year, but most shrews die within a few months of birth and never live beyond their second winter.

16

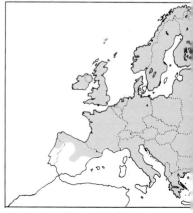

European Distribution

Pygmy Shrew (Order *Insectivora*)

Similar species: Despite its small size the Pygmy Shrew resembles the Common Shrew (*Sorex araneus*, page 14), the Greater White-toothed Shrew (*Crocidura russula*, page 20) and Lesser White-toothed Shrew (*Crocidura suaveolens*, page 22).

Field signs and clues: Because of their insignificant weight, 2–7gm (0.07–0.24oz), Pygmy Shrews rarely make an impression in the soil, unless it is very dry and dusty. Both tracks are minute, the forefeet measuring 4 x 4mm (0.15 x 0.15in) and the hind feet 5 x 5mm (0.19 x 0.19in). Five digits occur on each foot and there are distinct pads. Movement through the countryside is similar to the Common Shrew, but the average stride during the running gait is only 2cm (0.8in). The tail-drag is little more than a thread-like line.

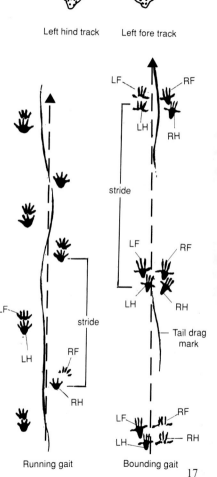

Left hind track   Left fore track

stride

stride

Tail drag mark

Running gait   Bounding gait

17

Water Shrew emerging from stream

British Distribution

WATER SHREW *Body length:* **6.3–9.6cm** (2.48–3.78in). *Tail length:* **4.7–8.2cm** (1.85–3.2in).

Neomys fodiens is the largest British shrew, with distinctive black upperside and silvery-white undersides, merging along the flanks. Bristly hairs grow on the underside of the tail and edges of the hind feet and assist paddling and steering whilst swimming. As with Common and Pygmy Shrews, the tips of the teeth are red.

Water Shrews are solitary outside of the breeding season, foraging constantly throughout the day and night in shallow burrows close to water. Burrows sometimes have underwater entrances and are found near clean rivers, streams, ponds and cress-beds, where the shrew hunts insects, worms, small fish and amphibians. Their saliva contains venom, sufficiently potent to partially immobilize the larger prey. Peak breeding occurs May–September, with several litters produced, each with 3–8 young. Absent from Ireland, some Scottish islands, the Balkans and Iberian Peninsula, Water Shrews are found elsewhere in the British Isles and Europe, although often the only clue to their presence is their high-pitched twittering call.

European Distribution

18

Water Shrew (Order *Insectivora*)

Similar species: In Europe the Miller's Water Shrew (*Neomys anomalus*) is similar, but in Britain the Water Shrew is the only species with black fur on its dorsal surface and silvery grey on the underparts.
Field signs and clues: Water Shrews are difficult to observe in the wild and the first sign is usually a line of bubbles rising to the surface of the river or stream. Air trapped within the fur glistens and makes the submerged shrew resemble a silver pebble, which bobs to the surface like a bubble immediately it stops swimming.

Water Shrews live in extensive burrow systems in the banks, with entrances usually just above water level. These burrows are well concealed and frequently it is the uneaten remains of fish, frogs and newts on the riverbank which first indicate the presence of this species.

Tracks are sometimes found in the soft mud at the river margins. All feet have 5 digits with the 2nd, 3rd and 4th pointing forwards, whereas the 1st and 5th splay at almost right angles to them. Pad markings can be very clear and whenever tracks occur the imprint outline is distinct. The hind feet measure 1.4 x 1cm (0.55 x 0.39in) and the forefeet 1.2 x 1cm (0.47 x 0.39in). This shrew moves with a running gait and the tracks are all splayed slightly outwards from the body and reveal a stride of about 4.5cm (1.77in) with a well-marked, broad tail-drag.

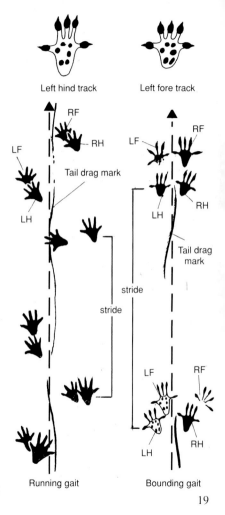

Left hind track   Left fore track

RF
RH
LF
LH
Tail drag mark
stride
Running gait

LF
RF
RH
LH
Tail drag mark
stride
LF
RF
LH
RH
Bounding gait

19

Greater White-toothed or House Shrew

British Distribution

GREATER WHITE-TOOTHED SHREW
Body length: **6.4–9.6cm** (2.5–3.78in). *Tail length:* **3.3–4.6cm** (1.2–1.8in).

    Crocidura russula is the most common of the white-toothed shrews, but in the British Isles is only found on Guernsey, Herm and Alderney in the Channel Islands. Central and southern Europe is its continental range. This species has grey-brown upper fur with a paler belly, and characteristic of white-toothed shrews, the ears are large and long and sparse hairs adorn the tail. The high mountain slopes of the Alps are colonized, but generally lowland habitats are preferred, especially dry grassland and hedgerows. Farm buildings and back gardens are regularly visited in search of insects, snails and small lizards. With a typical voracious appetite, nearly its own body weight of food is eaten daily. Because of a strong scent released from glands on the flanks and near the tail, this shrew is also called the Musk Shrew. The scent is used to mark their runs, as a deterrent to trespassers rather than as a means of following their own trail. The breeding nest is often built amongst boulders, where 3–4 litters of up to 6 young are reared.

European Distribution

Right hind track   Right fore track

Running gait trail similar
to that of Lesser
white-toothed shrew

Greater White-toothed Shrew (Order *Insectivora*)

Similar species: Some confusion can occur with the Lesser White-toothed Shrew (*Crocidura suaveolens*, page 22), wherever their ranges overlap. The Common Shrew (*Sorex araneus*, page 14), and Pygmy Shrew (*S. minutus*, page 16) also have similar features.

Field signs and clues: Because this shrew lives close to human habitation and is relatively abundant, it is often glimpsed scurrying through scrub vegetation and around buildings. Its predominantly grey-brown coloration and large ears are the first clues to identification. The nest is built of dry grass blades, moss and leaves and is hidden deep in grass tufts or beneath stones.

The individual tracks and trail are similar to those of the Common Shrew (*Sorex araneus*).

Lesser White-toothed Shrew on seashore

British Distribution

LESSER WHITE-TOOTHED SHREW
Body length: **5.3–8.2cm** (2–3in). *Tail length:* **2.5–4.4cm** (1–1.73in).

Similar in size to the Common Shrew, *Crocidura suaveolens* survives on Jersey and Sark in the Channel Islands and most of the Scilly Islands, where it is the only shrew. Southern and central Europe, east to the Black Sea, is its European distribution, but it is localized in France, Spain and Portugal. Resembling a smaller, Greater White-toothed Shrew, this species often forages on the seashore of the Scilly Islands, preying on sandhoppers and other crustaceans. Generally they prefer to hunt amongst boulders, under logs or in thick undergrowth concealed from predators, such as kestrels, weasels and cats. Territories are fairly small, ranging within 50m (164ft) of the nest. Breeding takes place from spring to late autumn, depending on climate. Up to 4 litters occur, each with 1–6 young, which are weaned after 3 weeks. Mature females are frequently pregnant again, whilst lactating their first litter. Juveniles can breed within a year, but often follow their mother around in a procession called caravanning, where each shrew holds on to the individual in front with its jaws.

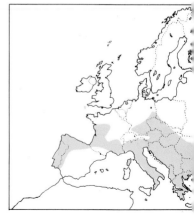

European Distribution

22

Lesser White-toothed Shrew (Order *Insectivora*)

Similar species: The most likely confusion is with young Greater White-toothed Shrew (*Crocidura russula*, page 20) or possibly the Common Shrew (*Sorex araneus*, page 14).

Field signs and clues: This species is elusive and more difficult to observe in the wild than most other shrews. Since it colonizes a variety of well-drained habitats, its tunnel network is found in dry surface vegetation, but the nests are always well concealed. The tracks are similar to those of the Common Shrew, but slightly smaller, and whenever they are found, the claw and pad marks are distinct. During the normal running gait, the stride is about 3.5cm (1.37in), but if the shrew is bounding the 4 tracks are grouped together as in those of the Common Shrew. A tail-drag mark is usually present.

Left hind track   Left fore track

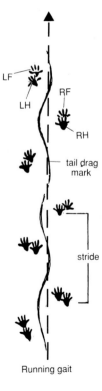

LF
LH
RF
RH
tail drag mark
stride

Running gait

Greater Horseshoe Bat at roost

GREATER HORSESHOE BAT *Body length:* **5.6–6.8cm** (2.25–2.75in). *Wingspan:* **39cm** (15.25in).

Rhinolophus ferrumequinum is a large bat with broad, rounded wings and short tail. Emerging from its roost 30 minutes after sunset, the wing-shape allows a slow, unhurried, butterfly-like flight, often low over the ground. The bat's mid and light brown fur with paler grey undersides is visible as it glides across pastures or along streams and riverbanks. Horseshoe bats get their name from a horseshoe-shaped nose-leaf around the nostrils, used for echo-location and visible when they hang upside down in caves, belfries and barns. This bat is one of Britain's rarest species, with a few hundred individuals confined to South Wales and South West England, but its range includes southern and central Europe, where it is still common around the Mediterranean. Mating occurs in autumn with a single youngster born June–August in communal nursery roosts. They start flying at 22 days, become independent at 35 days and reach sexual maturity at 3 years.

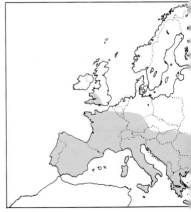

European Distribution

Greater Horseshoe Bat (Order *Chiroptera*)

Greater Horseshoe Bat hunting

Similar species: Its large size is a distinguishing feature, but the Lesser Horseshoe Bat (*Rhinolophus hipposideros*, page 26) has a similar appearance.

Field signs and clues: When they first emerge at night this species flies in dark, sheltered places. However, the hunting terrain always has sparse tree cover, where they catch large insects on the wing and even pick them off the ground or from other resting places. They fly low over water to drink or hover just above the surface before dipping their heads under. This bat presents a large broad silhouette against the sky. At rest, their pear-shaped bodies are characteristic and they hang free with their wings wrapped around them, but with their mobile, cone-shaped ears and face exposed. Adults possess pink or purple-brown wing membranes, whereas these are grey in juveniles. They are extremely sensitive to disturbance at the roost, twisting and turning their bodies immediately they become agitated. Night-time feeding roosts are often discovered by the accumulation of discarded wings and hard wing cases of moths, cockchafers and other large beetles. Alternatively, traditional roosts are identified by the presence of large quantities of guano or droppings.

Two Lesser Horseshoe Bats (left) and Greater Horseshoe Bat

LESSER HORSESHOE BAT *Body length:* **3.5–3.9cm** (1.25–1.5in). *Wingspan:* **25cm** (10in).

Rhinolophus hipposideros is a smaller, streamlined greyer version of the previous species with similar-shaped wings providing slow, highly controlled flight. Lesser Horseshoe Bats can hover and manoeuvre inside narrow chimneys and mine shafts only 50cm (20in) wide. They emerge from their roosts about 20 minutes after sunset, hawking gnats and moths throughout the night, around woods, scrubland and pastures, frequently near water. From its nostrils, this bat emits the highest-frequency sound pulse of any British species, which helps it locate prey as it moves its head from side to side during flight. It is an uncommon bat, restricted to south-west England, Wales and western Ireland. Throughout Europe its range is decreasing, but it is still found in south and central Europe, although almost extinct in Germany. Following autumnal mating, a solitary youngster is born in late summer of the following year. Horseshoe bats find it difficult to crawl because of their rounded bodies, so they require roost sites, into which they fly directly and sleep with their wings wrapped round the body like a cloak.

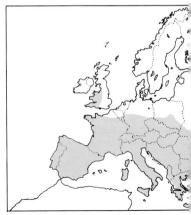

European Distribution

Silhouette of Lesser Horseshoe Bat

Lesser Horseshoe Bat (Order *Chiroptera*)

Similar species: Despite being significantly smaller, this species morphologically resembles the Greater Horseshoe Bat (*Rhinolophus ferrumequinum*, page 24).

Field signs and clues: Once mobile, this broad-winged bat is a skilful flier, often hunting only 2–5m (6.5–16.5ft) above the ground and rarely more than 10m (32.8ft). The bat's flight is recognized by abrupt changes in height and direction interspersed with short glides. Prey can be snatched from branches or off stones. Roosting sites include tunnels, caves, mines and old stone buildings, where they hang free and well spaced from their neighbours. At rest, their bodies are plum-sized and the wings are wrapped around the body, totally enclosing the face and ears. The wing membranes are characteristically shiny black. Like the Greater Horseshoe Bat, this species is easily disturbed at the roost, twisting and turning their bodies before flying off. Chirping, scolding calls are sometimes audible.

Daubenton's Bat at rest

British Distribution

DAUBENTON'S BAT *Body length:* **5cm** (2in). *Wingspan:* **25cm** (10in).

Otherwise called the Water Bat because of its regular habit of skimming over slow-flowing water, *Myotis daubentoni* is a medium-sized bat with reasonably broad wings providing rapid, quivering wingbeats. The upper fur is dark brown and buff-grey underneath with a short, broad, pinkish brown muzzle. Close observation reveals distinctively large feet with splayed claws. Emerging just after sunset, Daubenton's Bats patrol regular routes along woodland margins and rivers, frequently hunting at quite high altitudes, causing confusion with the Whiskered Bat. The communal summer roosts are usually crevices in masonry, especially under stone bridges, but tree holes are also used. Nursery roosts are typically in old buildings and are colonized by females only plus their single youngster, born June–July. During hibernation this bat becomes solitary, crawling into a crevice in a cave or wall during September. It is widespread throughout Europe and Britain, north to Inverness, but is localized in Wales and mainly found in eastern Ireland.

28

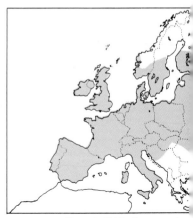
European Distribution

Daubenton's Bat (Order *Chiroptera*)

Silhouette of Daubenton's Bat

Similar species: This bat is easily confused with Brandt's Bat (*Myotis brandti*, page 30) Whiskered Bat (*M. mystacinus*, page 32), Natterer's Bat (*M. nattereri,* page 34) and Bechstein's Bat (*M. bechsteini,* page 36)

Field signs and clues: Uttering chirping calls during its rapid, circling flight, this bat is highly manoeuvrable on the wing. Wherever water occurs, it enjoys hunting 5–20cm (2–8in) above the surface without any abrupt changes in height, except to dip to the water to remove insects. It is even capable of swimming and taking off from the water surface. Sometimes the bat hunts for insects around trees 5m (16ft) above the ground, and occasionally rests in the branches between hunting forays. Standing on a bridge, spanning water and looking into the sunset is one of the best locations to watch Daubenton's Bat. They emerge after the larger Noctule (*Nyctalus noctula*, page 38) and generally before the smaller Pipistrelle (*Pipistrellus pipistrellus*, page 44).

When discovered at the roost, their short brown fur and dark brown ears, with tips curled backwards towards the fur, are characteristic features. The eyes are also encircled with pink skin and the hairs on the feet grow beyond the claws.

29

Brandt's Bat hibernating

British Distribution

BRANDT'S BAT *Body length:* **3.7–4.8cm** (1.4–1.8in). *Wingspan:* **25cm** (10in).

Myotis brandti is so similar to the Whiskered Bat that it was only recognized as a separate species in 1970. The fur on its back is reddish-brown, whereas that of the underside is buff. The muzzle, forward pointing ears and wing membranes are noticeably dark when closely examined and the feet are small. Juvenile Brandt's Bats are greyish-brown and very much like the Whiskered Bat, so that the only accurate diagnostic features are the shape of the male reproductive organs and slight differences in dentition.

Occupying similar woodland habitats to the Whiskered Bat, but also farmland and meadows, the summer colonies are located in old buildings, whereas they hibernate deep in caves. Much confusion surrounds the two species and the range of Brandt's Bat is still uncertain, although it appears to extend throughout England and Wales, but not in Scotland or Ireland. In Europe it is considered rare, but occurs in Norway and Sweden north to 64°, east to the Urals and south to Spain, but not Portugal.

30

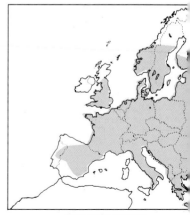

European Distribution

Brandt's Bat (Order *Chiroptera*)

Head on view of Brandt's Bat hunting

Similar species: The Whiskered Bat (*M. mystacinus*, page 32) and Daubenton's Bat (*M. daubentoni,* page 28) are likely to cause the most confusion in positive identification. However, Natterer's Bat (*M. nattereri*, page 34) and Bechstein's Bat (*M. bechsteini*, page 36) are also similar.

Field signs and clues: The wings are fairly narrow, providing a fluttering but rapid flight once they emerge just after dusk. Although they hunt as high as 20m (65.6ft) above the ground, most of the hunting is at low level, patrolling up and down hedgerows or close to trees. They are adept at performing tight turns around vegetation, but not so skilful as the Whiskered Bat in restricted spaces. At rest they often hang against walls, when the brown rounded ears are noticeable, together with the very dark brown face and wing membranes. A high, chirping and scolding noise is uttered if they are disturbed when roosting.

Whiskered Bat in crawling position

British Distribution

WHISKERED BAT *Body length:* **4.5–5cm** (1.7–2 in). *Wingspan:* **24cm** (9.4in).

Myotis mystacinus is difficult to distinguish from the Pipistrelle in flight and virtually impossible to separate from Brandt's Bat unless it is examined in the hand. It has narrow, pointed wings, with slower, more fluttering flight than the Pipistrelle, performed along hedgerows and woodland margins from sunset onwards. The upper fur is dark grey-brown with whitish undersides, but the muzzle, upright, pointed ears and wings are very dark. As its name suggests, long whisker-like sensory hairs occur at the corners of the mouth. During flight, like the Pipistrelle, the Whiskered Bat does not emit any sound audible to the human ear. Roosting in hollow trees and old buildings during the summer, the Whiskered Bat hibernates in caves and cellars during late autumn. Mating takes place in mild winter spells so that by the following spring the females are pregnant and give birth to a single youngster in June. Apart from northern Scotland, this bat is found throughout the British Isles and Europe, except Denmark and parts of the Iberian Peninsula.

32

European Distribution

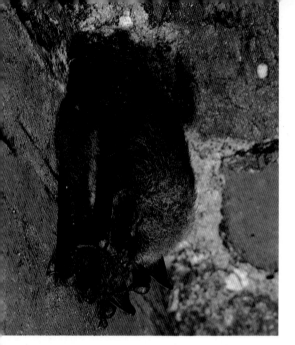

Whiskered Bat hunting

Whiskered Bat (Order *Chiroptera*)

Similar species: Positive identification from Brandt's Bat (*M. brandti*, page 30) is particularly difficult, but Daubenton's Bat (*M. daubentoni*, page 28), Natterer's Bat (*M. nattereri*, page 34), Bechstein's Bat (*M. bechsteini*, page 36) and the Common Pipistrelle (*Pipistrellus pipistrellus*, page 44) are similar.

Field signs and clues: This small bat is not easy to observe, but it emerges during early evening with a rapid weaving flight. It flies higher than the Pipistrelle, 1.5–6m (5–19.6ft) above parkland, gardens and around trees, hanging on to branches between flights. On warm spring and autumn days this bat even flies during the daytime to feed on midges and other small insects. At rest, the dark, shaggy fur and translucent, shiny wing membranes help distinguish it from the Daubenton's Bat. They hang free when roosting and rarely squeeze into crevices during hibernation.

Natterer's Bat showing aggression

British Distribution

NATTERER'S BAT *Body length:* **4–5.5cm** (1.5–2.25in). *Wingspan:* **28cm** (11in).

Myotis nattereri is a medium-sized bat, flying slowly with deep wingbeats on broad, pointed wings. Its white underside is easily distinguishable, whereas the back is grey-brown. Sometimes the long, drooping ears are seen; these are pink towards the base and brown at the tips. When resting or crawling, the long, bare, reddish face is noticeable, together with the baggy tail membrane with characteristic, outwardly curving margins and a unique fringe of stiff hairs.

On calm, warm nights, long after sunset, this species hawks for flying insects, frequently at rooftop height, but also along roadsides, hedgerows and woodland margins, where it snaps up insects from the foliage. During summer, breeding colonies, comprising females and young, form in hollow trees and quiet buildings. Juveniles are born June–July and fly by August. This species is widespread in Britain except northern Scotland and occurs throughout Europe except the Balkan Peninsula.

European Distribution

Natterer's Bat hunting profile

Natterer's Bat (Order *Chiroptera*)

Similar species: Daubenton's Bat (*M. daubentoni*, page 28) and Bechstein's Bat (*M. bechsteini*, page 36) cause most problems on identification, but Brandt's Bat (*M. brandti*, page 30) and the Whiskered Bat (*M. mystacinus*, page 32) are frustratingly similar.

Field signs and clues: This species generally emerges much later than any other bat and is at times difficult to see because it frequently flies between the branches of trees. The wings are clearly flexed during flight and the species is highly manoeuvrable, even hovering momentarily. Shrill calls are sometimes uttered during flight.

   At rest the ears curl backwards, but appear splayed when viewed head-on. The wing membranes are noticeably reddish. Natterer's Bats are often found hibernating in crevices, even lying on their backs, but summer roosts are frequently in the company of the Common Long-eared Bat (*Plecotus auritus*, page 46).

Bechstein's Bat is extremely rare

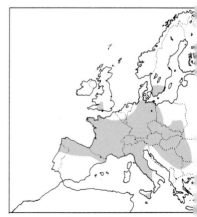

British Distribution

BECHSTEIN'S BAT *Body length:* **4.3–5cm** (1.75–2 in). *Wingspan:* **28cm** (11in).

Emerging soon after sunset, but only in calm, warm weather, *Myotis bechsteini* is a medium-sized bat with pale brown upper body and paler grey belly. The muzzle is long, narrow and pinkish-brown and apart from the Long-eared Bat, this species has the longest ears of any European bat, measuring 2.5cm (1in) long and extending well beyond the muzzle when held forward. Bechstein's Bat is one of Britain's rarest mammals, with only a few dozen sightings ever made, mostly in Dorset, Somerset and Hampshire. Its flight is slow and laborious, as it hunts amongst trees for insects, which are mainly caught on the wing or plucked from foliage. Males are typically solitary and little is known about breeding except that a single youngster is born in a small nursery colony generally inside a hollow tree. The species hibernates in caves, hanging head downwards so that the long ears hang loose and not folded up under the wings. In Europe it is found from northern Portugal to the Carpathians, with most sightings in Germany.

European Distribution

Bechstein's Bat (Order *Chiroptera*)

Bechstein's Bat swooping to feed from water

Similar species: Most likely to be confused with the Common Long-eared Bat (*Plecotus auritus*, page 36), but with shorter ears. All other *Myotis* bats are similar.

Field signs and clues: In good light the broad wings with their rounded tips and the long ears are usually visible. The wings do not appear to flex and are held rather rigidly, but the species is surprisingly agile in confined spaces and there is no audible sound during flight. It hunts for moths, beetles and mosquitoes rarely more than 1–5m (3.28–16ft) above the ground. At rest the ears are characteristically shiny and often curl backwards like miniature ram's horns. The wing membranes are translucent and brown, whereas the body fur is noticeably shaggy.

37

Noctule Bat in walking position

British Distribution

NOCTULE BAT *Body length:* **7–8.2cm** (2.75–3.25in). *Wingspan:* **39cm** (15.25in).

Nyctalus noctula is one of Britain's largest bats, strongly built and with slender, long, pointed wings which deliver rapid, shallow beats and enable the bat to fly quickly. The golden brown or chestnut fur of the adults is characteristic, but juveniles are darker. The short, rounded ears are black, whereas the face is dark brown. Emerging frequently before dusk, the Noctule often flies high in the sky with feeding martins and swifts and its high-pitched, squeaking call is fully audible. Corkscrewing dives towards the ground are regular, especially over its primary woodland habitat, although this species is often seen around parks in suburbia. Using cavities in oak, ash and beech trees as its summer roost, the Noctule is forced to compete with starlings, who also find such holes ideal nest sites. Tree holes are also favoured for hibernation, which occurs October–March. Apart from northern Scotland and Ireland, it is found throughout the British Isles and most of Europe.

38

European Distribution

Noctule Bat (Order *Chiroptera*)

Similar species: Leisler's Bat (*Nyctalus leisleri*, page 40) and the Serotine (*Eptisicus serotinus*, page 42) cause the most confusion in identification.

Field signs and clues: Noctule colonies are fairly easy to find in hollow trees and holes vacated by birds because the entrance to the roost is soiled by urine and bat droppings. They are also a noisy species and high-pitched twitterings and scoldings can be heard, even during the daytime. They are the first bat to emerge each evening and their silhouette is characteristic. Upon emerging, they fly extremely high and fast to a height of 200m (656ft) and often in a straight flight-path. The bats fly to their favourite feeding areas up to 6km (3.72 miles) from the roost, where they catch moths, beetles and other large insects during a hunting period of around 1.5 hours. Whilst hunting, the bat describes large circles against the sky, approximately 100m (328ft) in diameter and between 10–40m (32.8–130ft) above the ground. Occasional gliding sweeps are made to catch low-flying insects. Noctules frequently hunt in small groups, and the slow but loud echolocation calls can be heard by the human ear from over 91m (300ft) away. Other contact calls are given, including a short but piercing metallic squeal, which is painful to the human ear if uttered close by. If the light is good, the sleek golden fur is clearly visible, but the ears are inconspicuous.

Leisler's Bat asleep on tree stump

British Distribution

LEISLER'S BAT *Body length:* **5.4–6.4cm** (1.6–2.5in). *Wingspan:* **30cm** (12in).

Nyctalus leisleri is also called the Lesser Noctule Bat and is very similar to the *Noctule*, but is more brown or grey-brown than chestnut. The fur is not uniformly coloured and is much paler towards the tips. Leisler's Bat emerges just before sunset, flying high in the sky and catching aerial insects above the woodland canopy and across parkland. Unlike the Noctule, only shallow dives are made earthwards in pursuit of insects. During summer the males form bachelor colonies inside hollow trees, whereas the females form communal nursery roosts, where the single youngster is born between June and July. Tree holes are also used by both sexes for winter hibernation, which begins in October and lasts until late March. Throughout England, the distribution of Leisler's Bat is sporadic, although in Ireland it is one of the commonest species – perhaps even the stronghold of its world distribution. In central Europe its range is continuous, although fragmented in the west and nowhere considered common.

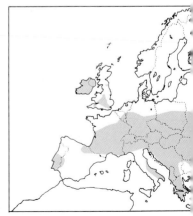

European Distribution

40

Leislers Bat in hunting profile

Leisler's Bat (Order *Chiroptera*)

Similar species: Noctule Bat (*Nyctalus noctula*, page 38) and possibly the Serotine (*Eptesicus serotinus*, page 42).

Field signs and clues: This fast-flying bat with narrow, pointed wings prefers flying just beneath the tree-tops rather than over them, although it does fly across woodland in the company of Noctules to a height of 30m (98ft).Whenever they are seen flying together, the smaller Leisler's Bats are more indecisive and wavering in their movements. The squarish ears are not visible during flight.

During summer roosting this species often squeezes into crevices, whereas in the winter they form dense groups and are recognized by their dark lank fur and bulbous faces. (Noctules always seem to retain their sleek appearance.) During autumn, male Leisler's Bats exude a characteristic pungent sweet smell which helps identification at the roost. Like the Noctule, this species utters loud, shrill calls audible to the human ear.

Serotine Bat eating prey

SEROTINE BAT *Body length:* **6–7.5cm** (2.25–3in). *Wingspan:* **36cm** (14in).

Eptesicus serotinus is one of Britain's largest bats, emerging about 15 minutes after sunset and flying slowly on broad, rounded wings. Frequently flying high above woodlands and parkland, this bat is often seen around buildings catching large moths and beetles on the wing, or making rapid, steep, vertical dives towards the ground. Serotines sometimes feed on the ground, crawling with forewings folded and hooking their thumbs into vegetation whilst pushing along with their hind feet. The dark red-brown fur with paler underparts, small, rounded ears and powerful jaws are easily identifiable and the tail tip projecting beyond the margin of the tail membrane is diagnostic.

Males are solitary, but females form large nursery roosts in roof spaces and hollow trees. The single youngster is born in June and becomes independent around August, when the colony disperses. Found only in southern Britain south of a line from the Wash to Aberystwyth, this bat is also found throughout southern and central Europe.

42

British Distribution

European Distribution

Flight recognition

Silhouette of Serotine Bat

Serotine (Order *Chiroptera*)

Similar species: Most likely to be confused with the slightly larger Noctule (*Nyctalus noctula*, page 38), but with experience they can be distinguished in flight. The Serotine is slower with broader wings, and whereas the Noctule has a wedge-shaped tail, the Serotine has a short tail membrane, which bears several points or may be completely round.

Field signs and clues: Upon emerging to hunt, Serotines fly straight in a level flight-path to their favourite feeding areas, which are within 1km (0.62 mile) from their roost. Like the Noctule, they can fly extremely high while feeding, but regularly hawk for moths and beetles just beneath the tree-tops at a height of about 15m (49ft). They catch their prey on the wing or snatch it from foliage while describing large loops in the sky along the perimeters of woodland. Once an insect is caught, the Serotine laboriously cruises around and dismembers the body to release the inedible wing cases and legs. The long, strong canine teeth leave 1mm (0.04in) diameter holes in the wing cases. If these are found on the ground they indicate that a Serotine feeding area is nearby. In good light the ears are discernible as a silhouette against the sky and the body fur appears very dark or black.

They are rarely found hibernating in winter, but the few species located have been inside cavity walls, disused chimneys and roof crevices.

Common Pipestrelle with young clinging to underside

British Distribution

PIPISTRELLE BAT *Body length:* **3.5–4.5cm** (1.25–1.75in). *Wingspan:* **19–25cm** (7.4–10in).

Pipistrellus pipistrellus is Britain's smallest, most abundant bat with reddish or dark brown fur, short, rounded brown ears and a snub nose. Pipistrelles fly from March to November, provided the temperature remains above 8˚C (48˚F). They emerge just after sunset, often feeding in suburbia over gardens and parks and uttering an audible, rapid clicking sound. Showing little concern for human presence, the Pipistrelle often flies low in a fast, fluttery flight, interspersed with twists, dives and spirals, whilst pursuing small moths, gnats and caddis flies. A regular route is generally patrolled, when the narrow wings are easily seen. However, they fly up to 5km (3 miles) to their favoured feeding grounds, so observation doesn't always mean a roost is nearby. Up to 1000 bats form nursery colonies in hollow trees and most frequently in buildings behind soffits and wall tiles. The young are born during June and July and fly after 3 weeks. Widespread throughout Britain, this species also colonises Europe south of 60˚N.

44

European Distribution

Silhouette of Pipistrelle

Common Pipistrelle (Order *Chiroptera*)

Similar species: Can be confused with Whiskered Bat (*Myotis mystacinus*, page 32) in flight, but is not so rotund in appearance and shows more rapid movements.

Field signs and clues: The small body, narrow wings and rapid agile flight assist identification. Usually they hunt 5–25m (16.4–82ft) above the ground and some 1–2km (0.62–1.24 miles) from the roost. When hunting over water, they skim barely 15–25cm (6–10in) above the surface where they catch gnats, lacewings and emergent mayflies. They are distinguished from the slightly larger Daubenton's Bat (*Myotis daubentoni*, page 28), which shares the aquatic feeding area, by their flight patterns. The Daubenton's Bat flies serenely and precisely across the water at a steady height of about 10cm (4in) from the surface, whereas the Pipistrelle flutters in an irregular, untidy fashion, occasionally leaping well clear of the surface before descending again.

Large roosts are identified by a liberal accumulation of droppings just below the access hole. These are deposited just as the bat flies into the roost in the early morning, and if the roost is in a house, the outside brickwork soon becomes discoloured. Pipistrelles feed intermittently throughout the night in 1–2 hour sessions.

45

Common Long-eared Bat crawling

British Distribution

COMMON LONG-EARED BAT *Body length:* **3.7–4.8cm** (1.5–2in). *Wingspan:* **23–29cm** (9–11.4in).

   Plecotus auritus gets its name from its huge ears, which are nearly as long as the entire body. Ultra-sensitive to sound, they can distinguish between an insect and the leaf it rests on. Emerging about 30 minutes after sunset, it is mainly a woodland species with yellow-brown or buffish fur, but paler underneath. Its broad wings and tail membrane are translucent, but provide a slow, controlled flight. With gentle flaps, the bat twists and turns among vegetation, hovering occasionally to snatch insects from leaves. Long, low dives are frequent, when the pale underside becomes visible and the silhouette of the ears are unmistakable.
   Summer nursery roosts contain up to 40 bats, usually inside a loft or under roofing tiles, where the young are born during June and July. Hibernation is in old buildings, trees and caves and occurs from November and March. Apart from Highland Scotland it is widespread in the British Isles and throughout most of Europe, except Greece, southern Italy and southern Spain.

European Distribution

46

Common Long-eared Bat (Order *Chiroptera*)

Silhouette of Long-eared Bat

Similar species: The much rarer Bechstein's Bat (*Myotis bechsteini*, page 36), although being slightly larger, causes the most confusion because of its long ears. The Grey Long-eared Bat (*Plecotus austriacus*), which is very rare in southern England but widely distributed in Europe, is extremely similar in appearance.

Field signs and clues: This species is perhaps the most graceful of all European bats in flight, but rarely flies more than 1km (0.62 mile) from its roost to feed. Moths form a large part of the diet and regular feeding perches are often first identified from a pile of discarded wings on the ground.

They regularly roost inside roof spaces of old buildings, where the long, thick fur is immediately obvious. Juveniles are a dull grey. The ears have rounded tips with distinct transverse folds and, when resting the bat curls them backwards and hides them beneath its wings. During hibernation, this behaviour probably saves heat loss through their huge surface area.

47

The localized Barbastelle

British Distribution

BARBASTELLE *Body length:* **4–5.2cm** (1.5–2in). *Wingspan:* **24–28cm** (9.4–11in).

Barbastella barbastellus is a medium-sized bat with glossy, dark brown almost black fur. The underside is slightly paler and older bats have cream tips to most of the fur, giving a 'frosted' appearance. The squashed, pug-like face and long, broad ears are black and the overall, strange appearance is unique. Regularly emerging before sunset, Barbastelles are intermittently active throughout the night and favour wooded river valleys, sometimes flying low over the water.

Males are solitary and smaller than the females, who form nursery roosts in buildings and hollow trees. Hibernation occurs in caves, cellars and mines, forming colonies of several thousand bats – often in mixed species.

Only a few Barbastelles are found each year, so its complete British distribution is unknown, although it is more common in the south and absent from Scotland and Ireland. It is rare in Europe, being sparsely distributed, and absent from Greece and much of Spain.

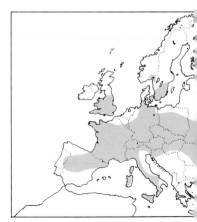

European Distribution

48

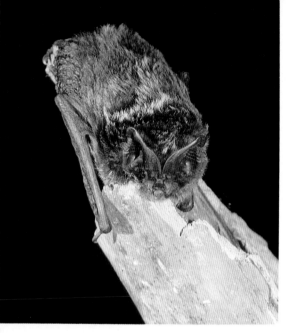

Silhouette of Barbastelle Bat

Barbastelle (Order *Chiroptera*)

Similar species: In Europe the Barbastelle cannot be confused with any other species, although when flying low over water they resemble the large Daubenton's Bat (*Myotis daubentoni*, page 28).

Field signs and clues: Since this is such a rare bat, little is known about its behaviour, but it flies low, usually 1–5m (3.28–16ft) above rivers with overhanging trees. Barbastelles circle just above the surface, suddenly rising to about 1m (3.28ft) before descending again. In silhouette the wings are broad and pointed and in good light the squarish head and ears are visible. The body fur and flight membranes always appear black during flight and only close examination reveals the large ears joined at the top of the forehead.

No breeding colonies are now known in the British Isles.

Young Rabbit outside burrow

RABBIT *Body length:* **34–50cm** (13.3–19.5in). *Tail length:* **4–8cm** 1.5–3.1in).

Oryctolagus cuniculus was introduced to Britain during the 12th century for their valuable fur and meat, but were released once rabbit fur became unfashionable. They are found throughout the British Isles and much of Europe, where large colonies are formed in grassland bordering woods and scrub, hedgerows, sand-dunes, sea cliffs and hillsides up to 500m (1640 ft).

Smaller than the Hare with shorter legs and lacking the black ear-tips, rabbits are greyish-brown with a rounded tail, which has a brown upper surface and white underside. When frightened the Rabbit bolts with its tail erect, revealing the underside as a warning to the colony.

Deep, interconnecting burrows form a warren, where 3 to 12 naked, blind young are born in special chambers during spring and summer. Up to six litters are possible annually, and early spring females can reproduce by their first summer. Mainly nocturnally active, rabbits feed during the daytime if undisturbed. Once alarmed, they frequently beat the ground with their hind feet and disappear into their burrows.

Similar species: The Brown Hare (*Lepus europaeus*, page 52) and Mountain Hare (*L. timidus*, page 54) in summer pelage cause the most confusion.

Field signs and clues: This is one of the easiest mammals to observe, and the numerous burrows on slopes and beneath hedgerows form warrens that are immediately recognizable. Wherever rabbits occur, horseshoe-shaped scrapes are common on the surface of the ground. They are generally silent animals, but utter loud distress screams whenever they are being chased or are captured by a predator such as a Fox or Stoat. Rabbits are herbivorous, favouring various grasses, succulent leaves and new shoots. Their feeding signs are obvious because the grass is closely cropped, producing a spongy sward. They also do large-scale damage to crops and bite off the growing shoots of young deciduous and coniferous trees, especially in winter. The shoots are

50

British Distribution

European Distribution

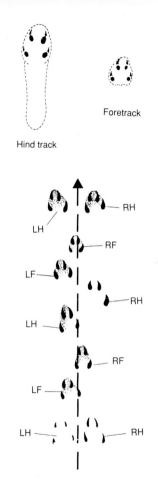

Hind track

Foretrack

RH
LH
RF
LF
RH
LH
LH
RF
LF
LH
RH

Hopping gait moving from hard to soft ground

Rabbit droppings

Rabbit (Order *Lagomorpha*)

ometimes left on the ground uneaten and the bitten surfaces are recognized as being caused by rabbits because they are obliquely cut and smooth-edged, as though sliced by a sharp razor. (Similar damage by a deer shows characteristically frayed edges.) Bark is gnawed from tree trunks, particularly when snow covers the ground. The tooth marks are distinctive; the Rabbit has four slender teeth in the upper jaw and two broad teeth in the lower jaw. In fact the two upper incisors are deeply furrowed, leaving behind a narrow ridge of bark in the tooth mark. The 1–1.25cm (0.4–0.5in) diameter droppings are very similar to those of the Brown Hare and are deposited randomly or in latrines on elevated ground, especially ant and mole hills or grass tussocks. The latrines are used as territory boundaries and the droppings are black-green when first deposited, weathering to pale brown within three weeks. Rabbits have five digits on their hind feet and four on their forefeet, but the fifth digit only shows in soft ground. The hind track measures x 2.5cm (2.36 x 1in), whereas the foretrack is about 3.5 x 2.5cm (1.37 x 1in), and although the digital pads do show up in certain soil conditions, often only the claw marks are revealed. If the entire foot from claw to heel leaves an imprint, the track may be up to 15cm (6in) long.

   Usually rabbits hop through their habitat so that the two hind feet land side by side and one fore leg lands slightly ahead of the other. The stride is around 20–30cm (8–12in). At higher speeds, when the Rabbit is bounding, the forefeet move closer together and the hind feet are moved in a leap-frog fashion, so that they land ahead of the forefeet. The stride then increases to about 80cm (31.5in).

51

Young Hares or Leverets

BROWN HARE *Body length:* **48–70cm** (18.8–27.5in). *Tail length:* **7–12cm** (2.7–4.7in).

The fur of *Lepus europaeus* is yellow-brown with lighter undersides and white belly, which can only be seen when the hare runs away. Apart from occasionally becoming slightly paler in winter, the Brown Hare's coat remains the same colour throughout the year. The black-tipped ears are longer than the Mountain Hare's and are held flat behind the head when resting. A shy, alert animal of open country, including farmland, downs and pasture, Brown Hares are mostly active in late evening or early morning, when they graze grass and other plants. The widespread use of weedkiller has deprived the Hare of its staple diet in many areas, but apart from Scotland and Ireland it is found throughout the British Isles and most of Europe, except the Iberian Peninsula. Whereas they can breed at any time of the year, mating typically occurs during March and April, when 2–3 leverets are born above ground in a form. Adults emit a shrill scream when threatened.
Similar species: The Rabbit (*Oryctolagus cuniculus*, page 50) and Mountain Hare (*Lepus timidus,* page 54) in summer pelage.
Field signs and clues: Unlike the Rabbit no burrows are excavated, but shallow depressions or forms up to 10cm (4in) deep are dug into the soil on cultivated land and used as day resting sites. Alternatively the form is made in long grass or undergrowth and only the ears and back of the head are visible once the Hare crouches inside. Hares leave obvious pathways through fields and open grassland and these well-worn routes often lead to a gap in the bordering hedgerow.

European Distribution

Brown Hare (Order *Lagomorpha*)

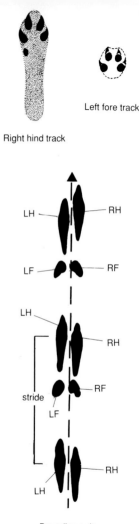

Left fore track

Right hind track

stride

Bounding gait

Like the Rabbit, hares sometimes damage agricultural crops and gnaw at tree bark, leaving marks indistinguishable from those made by the Rabbit.

Their droppings measure 1–2cm (0.4–0.78in) diameter, but are slightly flattened and more fibrous than those of Rabbits. They are variable in colour depending on the diet, but always grow paler with exposure to sun and rain. Droppings are deposited some distance away from the form often in small piles, although latrines are not used. They also occur randomly along Hare pathways.

The tracks are larger than those of the Rabbit with the hind foot tracks measuring 6 x 4.5cm (2.36 x 1.77in) and the forefoot tracks 4 x 3.5cm (1.57 x 1.37in). Whenever the entire hind foot from heel to claws is impressed, the track may measure up to 15cm (6in) long. Although the hind foot has five digits, the fifth is set so far back it only forms an impression in soft soil or snow. The forefeet have only four digits and the digital pads are clearly shown.

The trail is very similar to that of the Rabbit and varies according to speed of movement. During a slow hop the hind-tracks lie close behind the foretracks with a stride of about 25cm (10in). When bounding at speed, the hind feet are brought forward in leapfrog style, and are placed in front of the forefeet, and the stride may exceed 2.5m (8.2ft).

53

Mountain Hare in winter coat

British Distribution

European Distribution

MOUNTAIN HARE *Body length:* **46–61cm** (18–24in). *Tail length:* **4–9cm** (1.5–3.5in).

Lepus timidus changes colour with the seasons and in the north of its range, the winter coat is pure white with black ear-tips. In spring the coat turns brown but during summer, moults to grey-brown, and the blue-grey tinge to this coat gives the species its alternative name of Blue Hare. The tail remains white throughout the seasons and helps distinguish it from the Brown Hare's tail, which has a brown dorsal surface. Only in Ireland does the Mountain Hare remain brown all year although it is still greyer than the introduced Brown Hare with which it can be confused.

The hares feed at night on heather, bilberry and the shoots and bark of upland trees, especially birch. During the daytime they shelter in a den, which can be beneath the snow. Breeding takes place February–August, with up to three litters a year, each with 1–2 leverets. In Europe, Mountain Hares occur in the Alps, Scandinavia, Yugoslavia and the Soviet Union.

Mountain Hare (Order *Lagomorpha*)

Left fore track in snow

Left hind track in snow

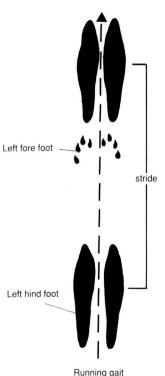

Left fore foot

stride

Left hind foot

Running gait

Similar species: The Rabbit (*Oryctolagus cuniculus*, page 50) and Brown Hare (*Lepus europaeus*, page 52).
Field signs and clues: Well worn trails through heather at altitudes of 300–750m/984–2460ft are usually the first sign of this species. The trails are maintained by the hares biting off the heather shoots and leaving smooth, obliquely cut stems, identical to those of the Brown Hare. The brown or grey-green circular droppings with a diameter of 1cm/.4in are indistinguishable from those of Brown Hare. Generally they are randomly deposited, but may be left in particular scrapes or on large flat prominent rocks. Tracks resemble those of the Brown Hare, but the hind-feet are heavily furred and in soft mud or snow they produce a broader imprint than those of Brown Hare. There are five digits on the hind-feet and four on the fore-feet. The trail is so similar to that of Brown Hare that it is usually the mountainside habitat which identifies it as belonging to the Mountain Hare. In the hopping gait, the stride ranges between 20–25cm/8–10in, increasing to 2 metres/6.56ft between each group of tracks when the hare is bounding at speed.

55

Red Squirrel in profile

RED SQUIRREL *Body length:* **19–28cm** (7.4–11in). *Tail length:* **14–24cm** (5.5–9.4in).

  Sciurus vulgaris is instantly recognized by its chestnut brown fur with white underparts. The bushy tail is also chestnut after the autumn moult, but in the British race it constantly fades, becoming pale cream by spring. The prominent, characteristic eartufts degenerate between autumn and spring. The tails of continental animals do not fade with the seasons. Preferring coniferous woods, especially Scots Pine, this species also inhabits deciduous woods, particularly beech, where they feed on seeds, berries, nuts, acorns and fungi. They do not hibernate and are active throughout the day, especially during the crepuscular hours, when they leap through the branches with agility. If alarmed, they flick their tails and make a 'chucking' sound.

  Dreys are built close to the main trunk and the young are born from March to September, with each female having up to 3 litters of 2–8 young. They become independent at 7 weeks. Present throughout most of Europe, it has declined in Britain as the Grey Squirrel has advanced, but it still found in Scotland, Wales, Ireland and part of East Anglia.

Similar species: The Grey Squirrel (*Sciurus carolinensis*, page 58) and Edible Dormouse (*Glis glis*, page 68).

Field signs and clues: Often descending to the ground, the tracks of Red Squirrel are clearly revealed in snow or soft mud. The hind foot tracks measure 4.5 x 3.5cm (1.77 x 1.37in) with 5 distinct digits and digital pads, together with a 4-lobed interdigital or palm pad. The foretracks measure 3.5 x 2.5cm (1.77 x 1in) with only 4 digits and digital pads. All the claws show clearly in the tracks. The usual gait is a series of bounding hops with strides of up to 1m (3.28ft) and the tracks arranged in groups of 4. The forefeet are always behind and inside the line of the larger hind feet. Whenever this squirrel is slowly searching for food, the stride is around 45cm (17.7in) and the tail is held erect, so no drag marks occur. Extended leaps of 3–4m (9.8–13.12ft) are sometimes made.

56

British Distribution

European Distribution

Red Squirrel (Order *Rodentia*)

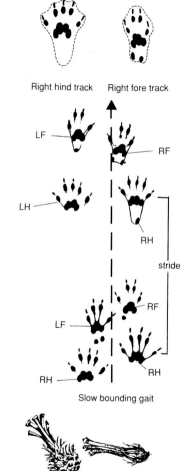

Right hind track   Right fore track

LF
RF
LH
RH

stride

RF
LF
RH
RH

Slow bounding gait

Chewed Pine cones

Scratch marks on tree bark in 3 parallel lines reveal where this squirrel regularly climbs into the tree-tops. These scratch marks often leave the bark rough and chipped. Red Squirrels also strip bark from the base, stem or crown of a tree – especially those 10–40 years old and often during the summer, when the trees are actively growing. Stem bark is frequently left hanging in ragged, spiral twists and the chewed terminal tips of branches are often left scattered on the ground in spring and summer. Although this species opens nuts in the same way as the Grey Squirrel, one of its favourite sources of food are fir cones, which are chewed in a characteristic way. Holding the cone in its forefeet, the Red Squirrel gnaws at the base, whilst the top of the cone points towards the ground. The small basal scales are loosely attached and easily torn off by the squirrel, which also tears off some of the cone shaft in the process, producing the familiar frayed cone. The harder, upper scales are removed by placing the cone on the ground, holding it steady with the forefeet and individually gnawing the scales as the cone is rotated. The internal seeds are eaten individually, but the squirrel leaves a few untouched scales at the top of the shaft, which produce a characteristic tuft. Depending on how close to the shaft the scales were gnawed, the discarded cone-shaft may be thick and frayed or thin and relatively smooth. At regular feeding sites, the frayed cones and stripped scales litter the ground, forming distinct piles. Like the Grey Squirrel this species gnaws at fungi and caches nuts and fruits just beneath the surface in late summer and autumn.

Red Squirrel droppings are round or cylindrical and vary according to diet, but are normally grey-black. They are similar in size to those of the Grey Squirrel and are randomly distributed.

57

Grey Squirrel feeding

British Distribution

GREY SQUIRREL *Body length:* **23–30cm** (9–11.8in). *Tail length:* **19.5–25cm** (7.6–9.8in).

Introduced to Britain from North America in 1876, *Sciurus carolinensis* is grey above and white on the belly, except in summer, when the fur has brown markings. The tail has white fringes and is noticeably bushy. Black individuals also occur.

The Grey Squirrel is the dominant species over England, north to Yorkshire, and is also found throughout Wales, lowland Scotland and north-eastern Ireland, although it is absent from all offshore islands. Both conifer and the preferred deciduous woodlands are colonized, together with parks and large gardens wherever large trees grow. Whereas dawn is the main period of activity, this squirrel forages for food throughout the day, spending much of the time in the tree tops but also searching for fruits, seeds, green shoots and roots on the ground. They sometimes steal fledglings or eggs from birds' nests. Circular dreys made of twigs and leaves are built high in the branches and breeding occurs from January to March and from May to July, when 3–7 young are born and reared exclusively by the female.

Similar species: The Red Squirrel (*Sciurus vulgaris*, page 56) and Edible Dormouse (*Glis glis*, page 68).

Field signs and clues: The shrill, chattering call of this species often announces its presence, especially when it is disturbed. The tracks are characteristic, but difficult to distinguish from those of the Red Squirrel. The hind tracks measure 5 x 3.5cm (2 x 1.37in) and there are 5 digits with distinct pad markings, whereas the foretracks measure 4 x 2.5cm (1.57 x 1in) with only 4 digits and obvious palm pad impressions. All the digits show distinct claw markings. Typically the squirrel moves in a series of hops, with all 4 tracks positioned close together and the hind feet turned slightly outwards and placed in front of the forefeet tracks. At a leisurely pace the stride is

58

No European Distribution

European Distribution

Grey Squirrel (Order *Rodentia*)

Right hind track   Right fore track

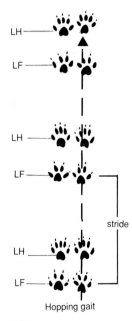

LH

LF

LH

LF

stride

LH

LF

Hopping gait

around 50cm (19.68in) but increases to 200cm (78.74in) when bounding at speed. Characteristically, squirrel trails usually start and end at the base of a tree trunk. Grey squirrels gnaw at tree bark, creating worn patches, which are regularly sprayed with urine. This forms noticeable dark and scented areas around the gnawed bark. The bark is frequently torn off in uneven strips and is dropped to the ground before the squirrel gnaws at the soft layers underneath. Bark stripping is performed on both coniferous and deciduous trees and if a complete ring of bark is removed from the trunk, part of the tree dies. Favourite feeding places, such as a tree stump or overhanging branch, are often used and remains of fir cones, nuts, berries and other soft fruits are liberally scattered on the ground around such perches. Grey Squirrels strip fir cones in a similar way to Red Squirrels, but the way they open ripe nuts is also instantly recognizable. Holding the nut firmly in its forefeet, the squirrel gnaws a groove across the top of the nut until a hole appears. The lower incisor teeth are then inserted into the hole and, in a crowbar-like action, the nut is cracked open to expose the kernel. Shattered nut fragments accumulate under trees where squirrels feed and cannot be confused with the signs of other feeding rodents. Sometimes unripe acorns or hazelnuts are eaten and the squirrel is able to completely decapitate the softer shell before extracting the kernel, so producing a different feeding sign. This species also feeds on fungi, and the circular caps strewn across the woodland floor always reveal distinct teeth marks. Grey Squirrel droppings vary in colour and shape, but are generally dark and cylindrical or round, up to 1cm (0.39in) long with 0.8cm (0.3in) diameter.

Hazelnut opened by Squirrel

59

Alpine Marmot occupy high altitudes

No British Distribution

British Distribution

ALPINE MARMOT *Body length:* **50–58cm** (19.6–22.8in). *Tail length:* **13–16cm** (5–6.2in).

Marmota marmota is one of Europe's largest rodents with greyish-brown fur which is paler on the underside. It has a heavily built rotund body with squat legs and large head, and is easily identified by its short but hairy tail and small ears. They are ever watchful, frequently sitting upright on their hind legs and sniffing the air for danger. Alpine Marmots utter a sharp whistle whenever threatened and rapidly disappear down their underground burrows, dug in south-facing mountain slopes above 1300m (4265ft). Only diurnally active, this species lives in colonies, where they communicate with high-pitched, piping calls. They are vegetarian, feeding on grasses, sedges and herbs, and using dry grass as bedding material. From October until spring, family hibernation occurs, several metres underground. Mating begins soon after awakening, with 2–4 young first emerging from their burrows in July and remaining with their parents until the following spring. The Alps remain the natural stronghold for this marmot, with other populations in the Carpathians, Pyrenees and northern Yugoslavia.

European Distribution

60

Alpine Marmot (Order *Rodentia*)

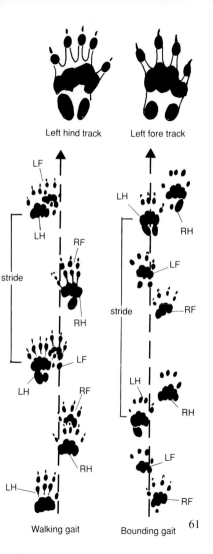

Left hind track   Left fore track

LF

LH

stride

RF

RH

LF

LH

RF

RH

LH

Walking gait

LH

RH

LF

RF

LH

RH

LF

RF

stride

Bounding gait

Similar species: The Alpine Marmot cannot be confused with any other mammal within its mountainous range.
Field signs and clues: The complex burrow and tunnel system with excavated mounds of earth near an entrance is the most obvious sign of marmots. The tunnels may descend 3m (9.8ft) below ground, but 1m 3.28ft) is more usual.

Marmots leave distinct footprints in the soil heaps around their burrows. The hind tracks measure .5 x 4cm (2.21 x 1.57in) and there are 5 digits, whereas the foretracks are 5 x 3.5cm (2 x 1.37in) with nly 4 digits. All digits reveal small oval digital pads with short detached claws. The 4-lobed terdigital (palm) pads of the forefeet are large and completely fused, but those of the hind feet are not so bviously joined. Two distinct proximal or heel pads occur in both fore and hind tracks, but one of the pair is articularly large in the hind feet and even merges with the interdigital pads. This creates a diagnostic feature marmot tracks.

During the normal walking gait, the tracks lie in alternate pairs, each pointing forwards. The stride easures about 20cm (8in), but increases to 50cm (20in) when the marmot bounds. During the bounding ail, the tracks occur in groups of 4 with the 2 hind tracks placed in front of the foretracks.

In densely populated regions, marmot trails are easy to locate since their runs wear deep into surface egetation. Main burrows are connected by regular trails to sheltered areas or feeding sites.

61

European Beaver showing flat tail

No British Distribution

British Distribution

EUROPEAN BEAVER *Body length:* **70–100cm** (27.5–39.3in). *Tail length:* **30–40cm** (11.8–15.7in).

Castor fiber is Europe's largest rodent, with stout body and flattened scaly tail. The dense fur is brown or yellow-brown and tawny-brown on the underparts. Strong legs, each bearing 5 claws, with the hind pair webbed, rapidly propel the beaver whilst swimming.

Beavers are active throughout the year and chiefly nocturnal, although disturbance causes diurnal activity. They inhabit wooded rivers and lakes, favouring alder, willow and birch. During winter, bark and twigs form the staple diet, but at other times trees are used to build dams or lodges. The huge, curved incisors are perfectly designed for felling trees, and a beaver can fell a 25cm (9.8in) diameter tree in 4 hours, whereas in winter, beaver families clear-fell over 300 small saplings. In summer various aquatic plants are eaten. Beavers usually mate for life during spring, and 1–4 young are born in June, remaining with their parents for 2 years. This species is widespread in Russia, but is only indigenous to Scandinavia, Finland and on the Elbe and Rhône. Elsewhere in Europe it has been reintroduced.

62

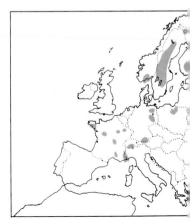
European Distribution

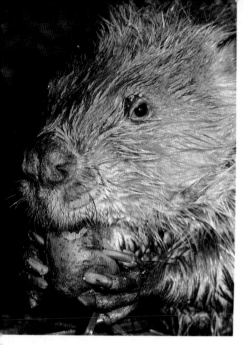

European Beaver (Order *Rodentia*)

Similar species: Possible confusion with the Coypu (*Myocastor coypus*, page 64).

Field signs and clues: Whenever they are alarmed, Beavers smack the water surface with their tails, producing a loud clapping sound. The dams, often up to 100m (328ft) long, built across rivers, cause large areas to flood, to that countryside occupied by beavers is easily recognized. Their lodges are immediately obvious and are very tall, with diameters reaching 15m (49ft).

The hind foot tracks are large, measuring 15 x 10cm (6 x 4in) with 5 digits bearing short claws which show clearly in soft mud The hind feet are also webbed and leave clear marks in the track. There are no webs on the forefeet, which also bear 5 digits and leave a track 5.5 x 4.5cm (2.2 x 1.8in). Sometimes a full heel outline shows in the mud. During the normal walk, when the stride is about 30cm (12in), the hind feet almost perfectly register in the track of the forefeet and the tail leaves a wide drag mark between the tracks. The tracks become less perfectly registered and the stride increases whenever the Beaver begins to run across soft mud. Beaver droppings are difficult to find because they are deposited straight into the water, but they are dark brown and only 2–4cm (0.78–1.57in) long. They are light and dry because they consist of coarse plant tissue and resemble hare droppings in consistency.

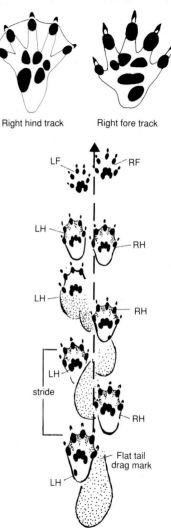

Right hind track   Right fore track

LF   RF

LH   RH

LH   RH

LH

stride

LH   RH

Flat tail drag mark

LH

Walking gait showing registration

63

Coypu in profile

COYPU *Body length:* **36–65cm** (14–25.5in). *Tail length:* **30cm** (12in).

Heavily built with a broad head, *Myocastor coypus* is a large rodent with coarse, pale brown outer fur, covering dense, softer fur underneath. The ears are small, but the incisors are large and orange-yellow. Short hairs cover the long, cylindrical scaly tail. All the limbs are powerful, especially the longer hind legs, bearing webs between 4 of the 5 toes and used effectively in swimming.

Originating from South America, the Coypu was introduced to fur-farms in Britain and Europe in 1929. Many escaped and established themselves along riverbanks, lakes and marshes. They prefer dense vegetation and in Britain became confined to the Norfolk Broads, where they dug burrows and tunnels into the banks, causing extensive damage. The Ministry of Agriculture attempted to eradicate the Coypu in 1988, but they are nocturnally active and elusive, so complete extinction is questionable. Entirely vegetarian, Coypus live in families, with 2–9 young born at any season, except during cold winters, when food shortage keeps populations controlled. Small colonies exist in France, Germany, Italy and Poland.

Similar species: Some confusion with the Beaver (*Castor fiber*, page 62), Muskrat (*Ondatra zibethica*, page 94) and Otter (*Lutra lutra*, page 116).

Field signs and clues: Large trampled areas close to river banks and surrounding marshland suggest Coypus are present. They excavate aquatic plants and cause widespread damage by digging out roots and destroying reeds normally used for thatching. Sugar beet and turnip crops are often plundered and any such crop gnawed by Coypu reveals characteristic teeth marks up to 1.7cm (0.67in) wide. This large rodent also creates short-turf lawns, by intensive grazing along

64

British Distribution

European Distribution

Coypu (Order *Rodentia*)

...he river banks.

    The tracks show considerable variation according to sex and age of the individual, but both fore and ...ind feet bear 5 digits with long, rounded claws. The hind track, including the heel, measures 13 x 8cm ...5.1 x 3.15in) with distinct interdigital and proximal pads. Apart from the inner digit, all the toes are ...oined by a web, which shows clearly in the tracks. Often a complete hand outline is revealed in the ...nud. The foretracks measure 6 x 5.5cm (2.36 x 2.16in) and the digits and claws are clearly visible, but ...here is no webbing. Both interdigital and proximal pads are revealed, but they are smaller than on the ...ind feet. Complete hand outlines are common. Usually Coypus move in a slow walk when the hind feet ...artially register over the forefeet and the stride is between 15–20cm (6–8in). However, this increases ...whenever the animal moves at speed in a series of bounding hops. The long, cylindrical tail produces a ...hallow scrape about 2cm (0.78in) wide generally to one side of the trail.

    Droppings are found at feeding sites or places where coypus leave the water. They are banana shaped, ...neasuring 3–4 x 1cm (1.18–1.57 x 0.39in) and are typically brown or green, bearing longitudinal ...riations when first deposited. Although often randomly left behind on the riverbanks, the droppings are ...lso deposited straight into the water.

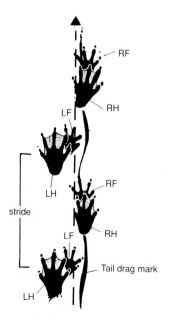

Right hind track   Right fore track

RF
RH
LF
LH
stride
RF
RH
LF
Tail drag mark
LH

Walking gait showing partial registration   65

Garden Dormouse foraging

No British Distribution

British Distribution

GARDEN DORMOUSE *Body length:* **10–17cm** (3.9–6.6in). *Tail length:* **9–12cm** (3.5–4.7in).

Eliomys quercinus is an attractive, nocturnal animal with large ears and characteristic black facial markings. The long bushy tail with white flattened tip is also diagnostic. Reddish-brown or reddish-grey fur covers the back, whereas the undersides and limbs are white. Deciduous and coniferous woodlands are the preferred habitats, but despite being extremely agile Garden Dormice are not as arboreally active as other dormice. They forage on the ground, amongst rocks and undergrowth, or hide in stone walls bordering gardens and vineyards. Omnivorous in its diet, fruit, nuts and berries are eaten, but insects, small mice and birds are also popular.

Garden Dormice are not found in Britain, but occupy most of central and southern Europe, except the Balkans. They hibernate from October to April, but breed during May, when 4–5 young are born in a nest built inside a hollow tree or rocky crevice. Second litters in late summer are common, and throughout their active months, Garden Dormice utter chattering, squealing calls.

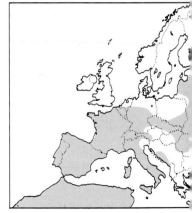
European Distribution

66

Right hind track   Right fore track

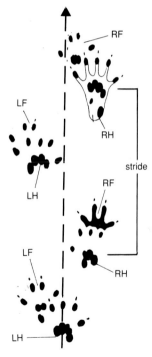

Walking gait showing registration

Garden Dormouse (Order *Rodentia*)

Similar species: The Edible Dormouse (*Glis glis*, page 68).

Field signs and clues: The most noticeable sign of this species are teeth marks left on stored apples. If they enter houses for hibernation, they often shred material into pieces for their winter nests.

Tracks are similar to those of Red Squirrel, but smaller. The hind tracks measure 4 x 3cm (1.57 x 1.18in) with 5 digits and accompanying digital pads. Both the 4-lobed interdigital or palm pad and the two proximal or heel pads show in the hind tracks. The foretracks measure 3 x 3cm (1.18 x 1.18in) with only 4 digits and digital pads. The interdigital pad is tri-lobed and there are 2 proximal pads, which are often obscured by registration of the hind feet. All the claw and digital marks are slender, which is a diagnostic feature of this species. The tracks are arranged in alternate pairs during the normal walking gait, with a stride of around 10cm (4in). During bounding movements, the tracks are arranged in groups of 4 with about 15cm (6in) between each group. Sometimes tail drag marks occur.

Edible or Fat Dormouse

British Distribution

EDIBLE DORMOUSE *Body length:* **13–19cm** (5.1–7.4in). *Tail length:* **11–15cm** (4.3–5.9in).

    Sometimes called the Fat Dormouse, *Glis glis* is Europe's largest dormouse, with grey or yellow-tinged fur and a squirrel-like bushy tail. A characteristic feature is the dark black ring round each eye.

    With a distribution similar to the Garden Dormouse, this species is found in central, southern and eastern Europe, but not the southern part of the Iberian Peninsula. In 1890 it was introduced to England, and is locally confined to Buckinghamshire and Hertfordshire. Deciduous woods are the favourite habitat, but mixed woodland, orchards and parks are increasingly colonized, and attics are used commonly for hibernation. Berries, seeds, fruit and tree bark are regularly eaten, but in some parts of Europe this dormouse also eats small birds and insects. During early summer, breeding nests are built high in the trees, sometimes using a hole in the trunk. 4–5 young are born towards midsummer, each with a life expectancy of 7 years. Winter nests are nearer ground level, with hibernation lasting from October to April.

Similar species: The Grey Squirrel (*Sciurus carolinensis*, page 58) and Garden Dormouse (*Eliomys quercinus*, page 66).

Field signs and clues: During spring this species becomes noisy at night, uttering whistles, squeaks and snuffling sounds which give its presence away. Whenever alarmed, the dormouse utters a threatening, churring sound. They are difficult to locate in the wild, but positive signs

68

European Distribution

Edible Dormouse (Order *Rodentia*)

include spiral strips of bark hanging from the upper branches of larch, willow and apple trees. This is common behaviour during April and May. Like squirrels, they often leave the remains of their food lying around tree stumps or beneath favourite branches. Unlike mice, the Edible Dormouse does not open nuts by gnawing a neat hole, but chews them, leaving an irregular, jagged hole before extracting the kernel. They are not split open like a squirrel feeding. The droppings vary in size and colour and are irregularly shaped.

Although small, the tracks of this species are quite characteristic. The hind tracks measure 3 x 2.5cm (1.18 x 1in) and there are 5 digits and small digital pads. The 4-lobed interdigital pad is often fused with the two proximal pads, but it is rare for the entire hand outline to be recorded in the track. The foretracks are minute, measuring 2 x 2cm (0.78 x 0.78in), and there are only 4 digits and associated pads. The interdigital pads are often joined, forming a central rectangle, and sometimes the complete hand outline imprints in the mud. The claw marks are always small or totally absent. During the normal walk, the feet turn slightly outwards and the hind feet partially register over the foretracks in a stride of around 8cm (3.14in). At speed, the dormouse bounds, with the tracks positioned in groups of 4 and about 30cm (12in) between each group. The bushy tail produces a distinctive drag mark around the tracks.

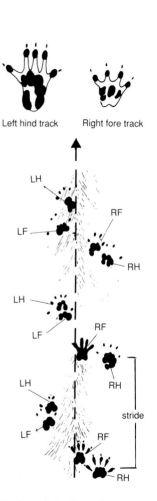

Left hind track   Right fore track

LH
LF
RF
RH

LH
LF
RF
RH

stride

LH
LF
RF
RH

Walking gait showing partial registration

69

Hazel Dormouse at base of hedgerow

HAZEL DORMOUSE *Body length:* **6–9cm** (2.3–3.5in). *Tail length:* **5.5–8cm** (2.1–3.1in).

   Sometimes called the Common Dormouse, *Muscardinus avellanarius* is a localized, declining animal in Britain, occurring south of an imaginary line from the Wash to mid-Wales. With orange-brown fur, paler belly, bushy tail and rounded body, this nocturnal and shy rodent is rarely confused with any other. They are arboreal, emerging at night to climb amongst the hedgerows, looking for fruits, flowers or insects, and even climb well into the woodland canopy, where they behave as miniature squirrels, leaping from branch to branch. Whereas hazel coppice is the favoured habitat, this dormouse is found in a variety of woodlands, parks, scrubland and orchards in Europe, but is absent from Iberia and some Mediterranean islands. Summer nests, usually built of stripped honeysuckle bark, grass and leaves, are built in shrubs well off the ground, whereas winter nests, where hibernation takes place between October and April, are often at ground level. Sometimes a bird's nest box is used for hibernation. 2–7 naked and blind young are born from May to September, and initially have grey fur before moulting. They leave the nest at a month old. *Similar species:* Some confusion with juvenile Garden Dormice (*Eliomys quercinus*, page 66) and possibly adult Harvest Mouse (*Micromys minutus*, page 72).
Field signs and clues: The main sign of this dormouse is large areas of honeysuckle finely stripped of bark and foliage to build their nests amongst dense vegetation. They also open hazelnuts in a characteristic way by gnawing a distinctive smooth, round hole fringed with

70

Hazel Dormouse (Order *Rodentia*)

Left hind track   Left fore track

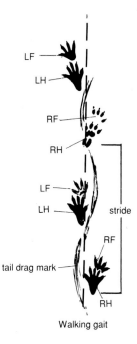

Walking gait

oblique teethmarks around the cut edge. (Wood Mice and voles leave cutting marks of their lower incisor teeth actually on the edge of the hole.) Opened hazelnuts therefore provide a definite clue to the presence of this dormouse. Ash fruits are also frequently gnawed to extract the seeds.

　　All tracks are minute; the hind tracks measure 1.5 x 1.1cm (0.6 x 0.43in) with 5 digital pads, but there are only 4 long digits with claws. The first digit is short and stubby and clawless. It is set well back in line with the 4-lobed interdigital pad. Complete hand outlines commonly occur. The foretracks measure 1 x 0.8cm (0.39 x 0.31in), with 4 digits bearing slender claws and 4 digital pads. All pads are very distinct and the 4 interdigital and 2 proximal pads form a circular pattern around the margin of the track, which often shows a complete hand outline. It is the shape and position of the pads which assist in positive identification of this species. During the normal walk, the tracks noticeably turn outwards and sometimes the hind feet partially register with the foretracks during the 7cm (2.75in) stride. The long bushy tail creates a familiar tail drag mark. When the Hazel Dormouse runs, the tracks are grouped together in fours with a stride of around 15cm (6in) between each group.

Hazelnut opened by Dormouse

71

Harvest Mouse in dense vegetation

British Distribution

HARVEST MOUSE *Body length:* **6..5–8cm** (2.5–3.1in). *Tail length:* **6.5–7.7cm** (2.5–3in).

As its name suggests *Micromys minutus* is Europe's smallest mouse with russet-brown back, white belly and long semi-prehensile tail. The small ears and blunt nose are characteristic features. An expert climber, this agile mouse lives among tall grasses and long-stemmed vegetation such as field margins, ungrazed meadows, scrubland and riverbanks with reedbeds. Harvest Mice are also benefiting from tall grasses on undisturbed motorway embankments. They are chiefly nocturnal animals, especially during the summer, but become active throughout the day in winter, emerging from nests built close to or below the ground. Grass shoots form the spring diet, cereal grain in summer and fruits, seeds, berries and insects are eaten throughout the year.

Apart from areas of the Mediterranean and Scandinavia, the harvest mouse is common in Europe and in Britain as far north as Yorkshire, but not on high ground.

Spherical breeding nests are built well off the ground, from neatly shredded and interwoven leaf blades, still growing on the plant. 3–8 young are born from May to September and become independent at 16 days.

Similar species: Some confusion can occur with juvenile Hazel Dormice (*Muscardinus avellanarius,* page 70) and Wood Mice (*Apodemus sylvaticus,* page 76).

Field signs and clues: This is the only British mouse to build 8–10cm (3.2–4in) diameter nests of woven grass, 30–60cm (12–24in) above the soil level, among stalks of tall vegetation. Summer nests are constructed in living tall grasses, herbaceous plants or shrubs, whereas the winter nests

72

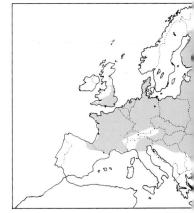
European Distribution

Harvest Mouse (Order *Rodentia*)

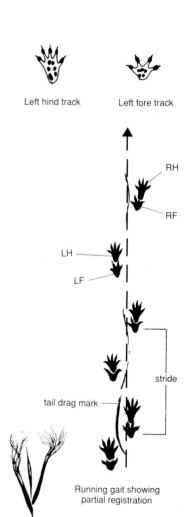

Left hind track   Left fore track

RH
RF

LH
LF

stride

tail drag mark

Running gait showing
partial registration

Grass frayed for nest building

e built amongst decaying grass tussocks or under tree roots or large stones. The highly characteristic
sts are most easily discovered during the autumn, when the leaves drop. During the summer, frayed and
redded grass blades, still growing on their stems but chewed to build the nests, indicate a colony of
arvest Mice nearby. The mice also chew at ears of corn during summer, but usually only those close to
e nest, so that such damage is difficult to detect in large cereal fields. Grain and seeds are stored near
e winter nests – especially those concealed in hay-ricks. Droppings are minute and difficult to find, but
e more concentrated around the nest sites. They are 0.2–0.3cm (0.07–0.11in) long and black-brown.
he minute tracks are distinguished from the similar tracks of shrews, because the latter have 5 digits on
oth feet. The hind tracks of the Harvest Mouse measure 1.3 x 1.0cm (0.51 x 0.39in) with 5 digits, digital
ds and long claw marks, whereas the foretracks measure 0.8 x 0.8cm (0.31 x 0.31in) with only 4 digits
d digital pads. Both tracks show a distinct arrangement of small interdigital and proximal pads and
mplete hand outlines are common. Typically Harvest Mice run with the hind feet partially registering
er the track of the forefeet and producing a stride of 3–4cm (1.18–1.57in). The tail produces drag marks
 a wavy line, between the tracks. Bounding trails do occur with the tracks in groups of 4 and 8cm
.14in) between each group.

73

Body detail of House Mouse

British Distribution

HOUSE MOUSE *Body length:* **7–10cm** (2.7–3.9 in). *Tail length:* **5.5–9.5cm** (2.1–3.7 in).

The fur of *Mus domesticus* is generally grey brown, but the species is extremely variable, although their tails are always long and scaly. Unlike other mice, the house mouse has a characteristic smell.

This species is widespread throughout Britain and Europe, where they live close to man in gardens, farms buildings, houses and factory sites. Elsewhere, cliff-tops, hedgerows and farmland are colonized, wherever food is plentiful. House Mice rarely move far from their food supply, which includes cereals, bread and fats, including cheese. They also eat obscure items such as soap and plastic and gnaw through electricity cables inside houses, causing a fire hazard.

House Mice leave characteristic droppings, and urinate over food, so becoming a serious health risk. Fortunately their maximum life span is about 18 months, but females have 6–10 litters a year, with up to 6 young in each. Within 6 weeks of leaving the nest, young females are able to breed.
Similar species: Juvenile Wood Mice (*Apodemus sylvaticus*, page 76) can be misleading.
Field signs and clues: In buildings, runways used regularly by mice are marked with greasy smears and urine stains. These pathways also have a characteristic stale, musty smell attached to them and are littered with food particles. Loop smears similar but smaller than those of the Black Rat (page 82) are also common. Wherever food is stored there is a chance the House Mouse will attempt to raid it. Cereal crops, vegetables and fruit are damaged, with grain showing

European Distribution

Left hind track

Left fore track

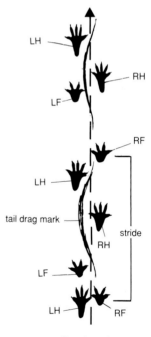

LH

RH

LF

RF

LH

tail drag mark

stride

RH

LF

LH

RF

Running gait

House Mouse (Order *Rodentia*)

...aracteristic teeth marks and powdered husks. Most food is ruined more by urine and dropping ...ntamination than by consumption. The cylindrical droppings are usually concentrated in favourite ...eas. They are 0.6cm (0.23in) long and 0.2–0.25cm (0.07–0.09in) in diameter and typically black, ...hough they vary according to diet. Outside of buildings the tracks are almost impossible to distinguish ...om those of Wood Mice. The hind foot is long and narrow, measuring 1.8 x 1.4cm (0.7 x 0.55in) with 5 ...gits. The 3 central digits point forwards with the other two positioned at right angles to them. There are ...interdigital pads and 2 proximal pads. One of the proximal pads is small and round whereas the other is ...al and much larger. The foretracks measure 1 x 1.3cm (0.39 x 0.51in) with 4 digits and is noticeably ...oad in relation to its length. There are 3 interdigital and 2 proximal pads, all of which are small and ...unded. Claw marks show clearly on all tracks.

    During the normal running gait there can be partial registration of the hind and foretracks with a stride ...f 4.5–7cm (1.77–2.75in). Whenever walking, the tracks are unregistered and point slightly outwards. An ...ndulating tail drag mark occurs commonly. Sometimes the House Mouse jumps with the tracks arranged ...n groups of 4 and up to 50cm (20in) between each group.

Wood Mouse or Long-tailed Field Mouse

WOOD MOUSE *Body length:* **8–10.5cm** (3.1–4.1in). *Tail length:* **7–9.5cm** (2.7–3.7in).

Apodemus sylvaticus is probably Britain's most widespread mammal, but because they are mainly nocturnal, they are rarely seen. The upperparts are sandy-brown, whereas the belly is white with a small yellow-brown streak on the chest. Their alternative name of Long-tailed Field Mouse indicates they are not confined to woodland, and this mouse occurs in gardens, on moorlands, mountainsides, cliffs and in hedgerows, even where ground cover is sparse. Apart from northern Scandinavia, Wood Mice are common throughout Europe. Food includes seeds, acorns and other nuts, insects, snails and worms. They are constantly active and their large hind feet propel them like small kangaroos as they leap away into the undergrowth. Territories are large and include their burrows, in which most of the daylight hours are spent. Food is also stored beneath ground in these burrows and they are used for breeding, with the young born in grass-lined nest chambers.

Wood mice are ever cautious when above ground, using their keen sense of smell and hearing to detect danger. However, many fall victims to owls, foxes, weasels and cats.

Breeding occurs from March to October, with up to 5 young born in each of the 4 litters. Few wood mice live longer than 2 years.

Similar species: The Yellow-necked Mouse (*Apodemus flavicollis*, page 78) and House Mouse (*Mus domesticus*, page 74) can cause misidentification.

British Distribution

European Distribution

Wood Mouse (Order *Rodentia*)

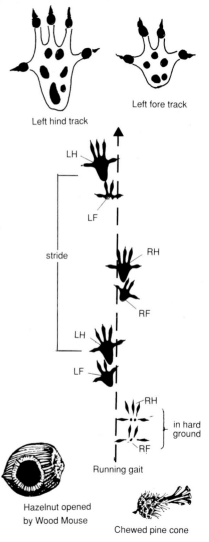

Left hind track

Left fore track

LH

LF

stride

RH

RF

LH

LF

RH

in hard
ground

RF

Running gait

Hazelnut opened
by Wood Mouse

Chewed pine cone

Field signs and clues: Wood mice are often discovered by food remains left around their burrows, on a favourite branch or tree stump or inside a disused bird's nest. Rose hips are chewed open to extract the seeds, but the flesh is discarded, and ash fruits have a hole chewed in the side where the seed is pulled out. Nuts are characteristically opened by gnawing a neat hole towards one end. As the mouse turns the nut around with its fore feet, the upper incisor teeth leave a row of small grooves around the edge of the hole. These marks are a diagnostic feature and are completely different to the gnawing signs left by the Hazel Dormouse (page 70) and Bank Vole (page 86). Wood Mice also strip fir cones very precisely. The scales are neatly chewed off because they do not have the strength of squirrels, who tear them off. A cone stripped by a Wood Mouse is therefore characteristically smooth and rounded, unlike those attacked by squirrels. Droppings are regularly found amongst discarded food remains. They are about 0.8cm (0.31in) long, rounded, pale brown and moist when first deposited, but darken and become dry with age. Although they are left at random throughout the territory, latrines occur at regular feeding sites or near the nests.

The tracks are larger than those of the Bank Vole and House Mouse, with the hind tracks measuring 2.2 x 1.8cm (0.86 x 0.7in) and the foretracks 1.3 x 1.5cm (0.5 x 0.6in). There are 5 digits and associated digital pads in the hind tracks and the claw marks are long. The 4 interdigital and 2 proximal pads show clearly and the tracks often reveal a complete hand outline. The foretracks have 4 digits and digital pads but only 3 interdigital pads. The two proximal pads vary – one is circular, the other elongated. All the digits splay widely in their tracks. During the normal running gait the hind feet partially register over the foretracks with a stride between 8–10cm (3.2–4in). Bounds of 15cm (6in) are common, with tracks arranged in groups of 4, sometimes with a tail drag showing between the tracks.

Yellow-necked Mouse showing body detail

British Distribution

YELLOW-NECKED MOUSE *Body length:* **9–13cm** (3.5–5.1in). *Tail length:* **9–13.5cm** (3.5–5.3in).

Apodemus flavicollis resembles a large Wood Mouse, with richer brown upperparts and orangey flanks. When sitting upright, the yellow-brown, collar-shaped patch is visible on the chest.

Yellow-necked mice occupy woodlands, hedgerows and wooded gardens, but have a localized distribution in England and Wales. They share the same habitats with Wood Mice wherever their distributions overlap, but are more agile and are found climbing high into bushes in search of young buds. The diets of both mice are similar, but Yellow-necked Mice often raid apple stores in attics and outbuildings.

Absent from northern and western Europe, this mouse is common elsewhere east to the Urals and even over 2000m (6562ft.) in the Alps.

Breeding begins as early as February, with the nest constructed from grass and leaves and hidden under tree stumps or roots; alternatively underground in the burrow. Up to 3 litters are possible, with 3–5 young in each, becoming independent at 18 days.

78

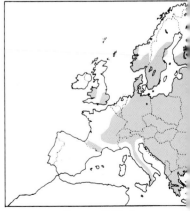

European Distribution

Yellow-necked Mouse (Order *Rodentia*)

Similar species: The Wood Mouse (*Apodemus sylvaticus*, page 76).
Field signs and clues: The Yellow-necked Mouse is a more adept climber than the Wood Mouse, and especially during winter it climbs high into shrubs and saplings and gnaws the developing buds. Diagnostic signs include holes chewed in the side of buds with their insides scraped out by the sharp incisors of the mouse. Other field signs left by this species are impossible to distinguish from the Wood Mouse, since they gnaw fruits, nuts and cones in the same way. Even their tracks are very similar, but those of the Yellow-necked Mouse are slightly larger. The hind tracks measure 2 x 1.9cm (0.78 x 0.74in) with 6 distinct pad imprints and the proximal pair set well back on the heel. The foretracks measure 1.6 x 1.8cm (0.62 x 0.71in) with 3 interdigital and 2 proximal pads. All the claw marks show clearly and generally tracks of this species are more deeply impressed than those of the Wood Mouse, although this is not a reliable means of differentiation. The two species cannot be reliably distinguished on the basis of their trails, since both move in similar gaits. A stride of 4.5–5cm (1.77–1.96in) is common and the tracks show a distinct digital splay with occasional tail drag, although this is normally held clear of the ground. It is the restricted distribution of the Yellow-necked Mouse throughout its range that suggests that it might be responsible for certain field signs. However, once seen, the mouse is recognized by its larger size, darker upper fur and longer tail. It is also typically more agile.

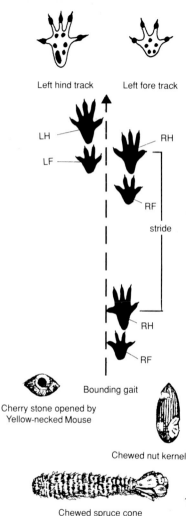

Left hind track   Left fore track

LH
LF   RH

                   RF

                   stride

                   RH

                   RF

Bounding gait

Cherry stone opened by
Yellow-necked Mouse

Chewed nut kernel

Chewed spruce cone

79

Brown Rats eating grain in farmyard

BROWN RAT *Body length:* **11–29cm** (4.3–11.4in). *Tail length:* **8.5–23cm** (3.35–9in).

Rattus norvegicus is a widespread pest and is also called the Common Rat, having spread to Europe from Asia in the Middle Ages and reaching Britain in the 18th century. They are usually brown with greyer underparts, but Black individuals do occur, and apart from their shorter, thicker tail and rounder muzzle can be confused with the Black Rat.

Brown Rats are highly adaptable and great opportunists, so have colonized all man-made habitats, including farmland and buildings, rubbish tips, sewers, factory sites, railway yards and disused cellars. Elsewhere they thrive along river banks, estuaries and coastlines, where they raid eggs from nesting seabird colonies.

They are mainly nocturnal, efficient swimmers and climbers, and feed on almost anything from household waste to root crops and fruit. Wherever food and shelter are available, females breed throughout the year, producing up to 50 young in 5–6 litters. The young are able to breed within 3 months, but fortunately many are killed by cats, owls, weasels and man.
Similar species: The Black Rat (*Rattus rattus*, page 82) and Water Vole (*Arvicola terrestris*, page 92) can cause misidentification.
Field signs and clues: Regularly used pathways in grass or across mud are the first indication of this species. They are 5–10cm (1.96–3.9in) wide and frequently lead to burrows with entrances 6–10cm (2.36–3.9in) in diameter in the side of a bank or ditch or beneath rocks and tree roots. As with Black Rats, they create dark greasy patches where their bodies rub against surfaces inside buildings. Brown Rats chew on anything, including stored grain, root crops, woodwork, pipes,

European Distribution

Brown Rat (Order *Rodentia*)

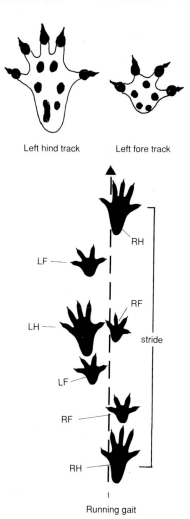

Left hind track   Left fore track

RH

LF

RF

LH

stride

LF

RF

RH

Running gait

soap, plastic and food remains and the gnawing marks are immediately obvious. Around farms, they extensively damage stored hay stacks and heavily stain them with their urine and greasy fur.

Brown Rats produce around 40 droppings daily, each measuring 1.7–2cm (0.66–0.78in) long and 0.2–0.3cm (0.07–0.11in) in diameter. They are coarse in texture and vary in colour depending on the diet, but have characteristically pointed ends. Regular latrine sites are used, including rafter joints in roof spaces.

The tracks resemble those of the Black Rat and are similar to those of the Water Vole. Hind tracks measure 3.3 x 2.8cm (1.29 x 1.1in) with 5 digits and associated pads. The inner and outer digits splay at right angles to the 3 forwardly pointing digits. There are 4 equally spaced interdigital pads and 2 proximal pads, one of which is noticeably elongated. The hind tracks generally show a long heel area. The foretracks measure 1.8 x 2.5cm (0.7 x 1in) with 4 digits and clearly impressed digital pads. The interdigital and proximal pads form a distinct pattern around the margins of the tracks, which often show a complete hand outline. Both fore and hind tracks clearly show the large claw marks. When running, the tracks point slightly outwards and there is partial registration between hind and forefeet with a stride of 10–15cm (4–6in). Whenever bounding, the tracks occur in groups of 4, with up to 60cm (24in) between each group. Tail drag marks are rare, but they do occur in dusty grain stores.

Body detail of Black Rat

BLACK RAT *Body length:* **9.5–24cm** (3.7–9.5in). *Tail length:* **11.5–26cm** (4.5–10in).

Famed for its part in carrying plague, *Rattus rattus* is identified by its uniformly dark tail, which is longer than its body. The common black form does not guarantee identification, since some black or ship rats are actually brown. It is smaller, more streamlined than the Common Rat and the large, rounded pink ears are characteristic.

Originally from India, the Black Rat is found throughout the Mediterranean and central Europe, but is declining elsewhere. In Britain it is now scarce, chiefly confined to main ports and old coastal towns, where they forage inside warehouses and disused buildings. This species is generally associated with human habitation, but farmland is also colonized. They are mostly nocturnal and extremely agile, climbing ropes and brickwork, and regularly gnaw their way into wooden buildings to eat grain and fruit stores. Between March and November, 3–5 litters are born, each with 6–7 young, which mature within 4 months. The nest is built above ground, in cavity walls, in between rafters or even in hollow trees.

Similar species: Sometimes mistaken for dark forms of the Brown Rat (*Rattus norvegicus*, page 80).
Field signs and clues: Well-worn runways in grass or bare earth up to 10cm (3.9in) wide indicate the presence of this species. Burrows similar to those of the Brown Rat are sometimes excavated. Since this species is largely confined to warehouses and buildings with cavity walls and ceilings, where it moves unseen, gnawed woodwork, pipes and insulating material are frequently observed. Greasy smears occur in places where the rats pass regularly and where movement is restricted, causing the fur to rub against the wall or woodwork and leaving a black mark. Diagnostic "loop"

82

Black Rat (Order *Rodentia*)

Left hind track   Left fore track

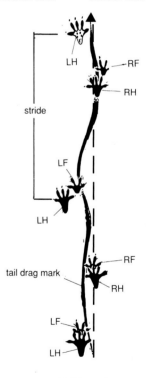

stride

tail drag mark

LH

RF

RH

LF

LH

RF

RH

LF

LH

Walking gait

smears are common and these semicircular marks occur on vertical surfaces or under beams, girders and pipes, where the rat swings to continue its journey.

Their droppings are smaller than those of Brown Rats and are generally narrower, slightly curved and rounded at the ends. Measuring 1–1.2cm (0.39–0.47in) long and 0.2–0.3cm (0.07–0.12in) in diameter, they vary in colour and in buildings are deposited randomly across the floor, whereas, in the same habitat, Brown Rats deposit their droppings in corners or along the edge of walls. The droppings of the two species can be distinguished with accuracy on their diameter (d) to length (l) ratio. If d/l is between 0.31–0.37, the droppings belong to the Black Rat. If the d/l is 0.42–0.46, they belong to the Brown Rat.

The tracks are virtually indistinguishable from those of the Brown Rat. Hind-tracks measure 2.5 x 2.5cm (1 x 1in) with 5 digits and digital pads. The 3 central digits point forwards, whereas the inner and outer digits are at right angles to these. The 4 interdigital and 2 proximal pads are generally distinct. The foretracks measure 1.5 x 2cm (0.59 x 0.78in) with 4 digits and digital pads. The 3 interdigital and 2 proximal pads form a pattern around the track margin. Complete hand outlines show commonly in both tracks and the claw marks are always distinct. During the normal running trail, the hind feet partially register over the foretracks with a stride of 8–10cm (3.2–4in). A continuous tail drag regularly occurs. When bounding, the tracks occur in groups of 4 with up to 50cm (20in) between each group.

83

Norway Lemming

British Distribution

NORWAY LEMMING *Body length: 13–15cm* (5.1–6in). *Tail length: 1.5–1.9cm* (0.6–0.75in).

The black, yellow and yellow brown fur of *Lemmus lemmus* make it unmistakable even when quickly disappearing into its burrow. A squat body, short legs, stumpy tail and small rounded ears are further characteristic features of this gregarious vegetarian rodent, which occurs throughout Scandinavia and Norway, east to the Kola Peninsula. Tundra above 1000m (3281ft) is the preferred habitat, but birch and willow scrubland are regularly colonized. Living in a network of subterranean burrows, lemmings are active day and night throughout the year. Unlike other rodents, they do not hop, but run quickly and swim effectively. Every fourth year, lemming populations peak and the famous mass migrations occur, during which they utter loud hisses and squeals. They become totally disorganized and even attempt to swim across wide bays, drowning in their attempts to reach dry land. It is entirely mythical that lemmings show suicidal tendencies and intentionally jump over cliffs. Breeding occurs from April to October, with 2–13 young born and becoming independent around 3 weeks old.

European Distribution

84

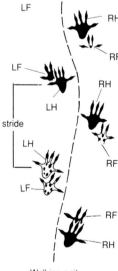

Left hind track   Left fore track

LH
LF
RH
RF
LF
RH
LH
stride
LH
RF
LF
RF
RH

Walking gait

Norway Lemming (Order *Rodentia*)

Similar species: Cannot be confused with any other mammal within its range.

Field signs and clues: Lemming pathways and runs through low-growing vegetation are relatively easy to find. Their droppings are deposited in piles along these regular routes and are light brown, cylindrical with rounded ends and between 0.3–0.8cm (0.11–0.31in) long. They can be confused with droppings of the Field Vole (*Microtus agrestis*, page 88). Lemming tracks are similar to other voles. They are minute with 5 digits and digital pads on the hind feet and with the interdigital and proximal pads arranged in a distinct pattern around the margins of the tracks. The forefeet have 4 digits and associated pads and the distinctly separated interdigital and proximal pads show clearly in the tracks. Complete hand outlines are often revealed and the claw marks are noticeably long – especially in winter. The claw marks are a diagnostic feature of the Norway Lemming tracks. During a slow walk the hind feet partially register over the tracks of the forefeet with a stride of around 8cm (3.14in). Because of their short legs, body drag marks frequently occur throughout the trail, and the Norway Lemming is unique among rodents because it never walks in a straight line, but moves from left to right, producing a trail in a snake-like meandering line.

A pair of Bank Voles

British Distribution

BANK VOLE *Body length:* **8–13.5cm** (3.15–5.3in). *Tail length:* **3.5–7cm** (1.3–2.7in).

When fully grown, *Clethrionomys glareolus* has shiny chestnut-brown upper fur, with greyish underparts and a two-coloured tail, where the dorsal surface is brown. Young bank voles are grey-brown and can be confused with Field Voles. Active by day and night throughout the year, Bank Voles scurry along regular surface runs or underground burrows in woodland, bramble thickets, hedgerows, moorland and large gardens. Only south-western Ireland is colonized, but elsewhere in the British Isles the Bank Vole is one of the most common mammals. Equally in Europe, the Mediterranean countries are sparsely populated, but the vole is common in central and most northern countries.

The Vole feeds on a variety of seeds, fruits, buds and leaves, adeptly climbing into the branches of shrubs and trees. Berries and nuts are stored in the burrows, ready for the winter. Breeding nests made from leaves, grass and moss are built in tree crevices, in dense undergrowth, or below ground, and between April and October, 3–5 young are born in several litters.
Similar species: The Field Vole (*Microtus agrestis*, page 88) and Common Vole (*Microtus arvalis*, page 90) are confusing.
Field signs and clues: Sometimes the adults can be heard emitting a high-pitched squeak, but usually it is the extensive surface runways and burrows in thick vegetation which give the rodent's presence away. Tunnels disappear below ground to a depth of 2–10cm (0.78–4in) and food remains are often seen around the entrances. Bank Voles actively gnaw bark of conifers and soft deciduous trees and shrubs such as elderberry. The bark is completely stripped from large areas of the branches so that they appear white and are particularly noticeable during autumn and winter. Since they are agile climbers, the gnawing extends several metres up into the branches and even trees with trunk diameters of 30cm (12in) are attacked. Gnawing begins where the

European Distribution

Bank Vole (Order *Rodentia*)

Left hind track   Left fore track

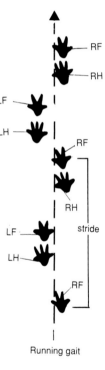

Running gait

branches meet the trunk, because the vole can easily sit in this position. The remains of the bark are left as a thin brown layer, finely furrowed by the vole's teeth, with grooves measuring 0.2cm (0.078in) wide. Bank Voles also gnaw holes in tree buds similar to those of the Yellow-necked Mouse (page 78). Hazlenuts and acorns are characteristically gnawed open with a neat circular hole with no teeth marks on the outer edge like Wood Mice, although there may be some incisor grooves on the inner rim of the hole. Similar grooves are found on the edge of fungi nibbled by this species. Bank Voles enjoy eating rose hips, but in contrast to Wood Mice, they eat the flesh and discard the seeds. Berries and nuts are regularly carried and stored in old birds' nests, but tunnels or holes under stones are also used as caches. The droppings are frequently deposited in small groups and are much narrower than those of Wood Mice with a diameter of 0.4cm (0.15in). They are rounded in section and up to 0.8cm (0.31in) long and dark brown or black when first deposited. Their colour varies according to diet, but they lack the green coloration of Field Vole droppings (page 88).

The tracks are minute, the hind tracks measuring 1.5 x 1.7cm (0.59 x 0.66in) with 5 digits and digital pads. The 3 middle digits point forwards, but the 2 outer digits are splayed at right angles, producing a star-shaped track. The foretracks measure 1.1 x 1.3cm (0.43 x 0.51in) with only 4 digits and digital pads. Although complete hand outlines are common, the claw marks do not always show in the tracks. During the normal running gait, the tracks do not register but produce a stride of 6–7cm (2.36–2.75in) and there is no tail drag. When bounding the tracks occur in groups of 4 with 15cm (5.9in) between each group.

Hazelnut opened by Bank Vole

87

Field or Short-tailed Vole

British Distribution

FIELD VOLE *Body length:* **7.5–13.5cm** (2.9–5.3in). *Tail length:* **1.8–5cm** (0.7–1.9in).

The shaggy, yellow-brown fur of *Microtus agrestis* is characteristic, with paler grey undersides and paws. It has small ears and a blunt nose, typical of all voles, but the tail is pinker than other species and it is also called the Short-tailed Vole. Belligerent and constantly squeaking and chattering, this species is highly territorial, driving other voles from their runways in rough grassland, meadows, hedgerows, marshes and woodland. In the Alps they live at altitudes of 1900m (6230ft). Apart from Ireland this species is widespread in the British Isles and is equally common in Europe, except Spain, Italy and Greece.

Succulent grass stems form the main diet, but roots, bulbs and bark are eaten, especially in winter. Extensive tunnels and nest chambers are built amongst grass stems and below the surface. They are prolific breeders and between March and December 4–5 litters, each with up to 6 young, are reared. Within 6 weeks young females can breed and sometimes plague numbers occur. They fall prey to owls, foxes and weasels and few survive longer than a year.

Similar species: The Bank Vole (*Clethrionomys glareolus*, page 86) and Common Vole (*Microtus arvalis*, page 90) can be confusing.

Field signs and clues: Loud chattering noises are heard when several voles meet within their territory and draw attention to the complex network of runways at suface level amongst dense grass. Recent use of runs is indicated by the presence of droppings and chopped grass leaves and

88

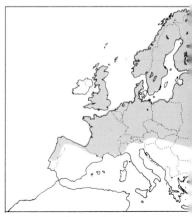

European Distribution

Left hind track

Left fore track

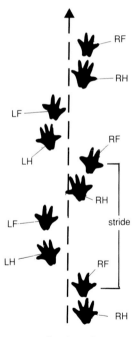

Running gait

eld Vole (Order *Rodentia*)

ems littering the route. Like the Bank Vole, this species strips sapling bark during the winter,
ncentrating on the lowest 10–15cm (3.9–6in) of the trunk and lower branches. This species has stronger
eth, so that the bark is completely gnawed off, leaving clear incisor grooves in the wood below. Bark
awing is often confined to small areas of the trunk so that the sapling becomes completely ringed and
es. Field Voles also damage young trees by gnawing through their root systems below ground. The oval
oppings, which are mostly found near the vole's tunnels and runways, are characteristically green
cause of the high content of grass in the diet. They are about 0.6cm (0.23in) long. The tracks reveal the
pical star-shaped digit formation of voles. Hind tracks measure 1.5 x 1.8cm (0.59 x 0.70in) with five
gits and digital pads. The short claws are usually visible as are the 4 interdigital and 2 proximal pads.
e foretracks are 1.2 x 1.5cm (0.47 x 0.59in) with only four digits and associated pads. The claw marks
e very short, but the three interdigital and two proximal pads usually show clearly. Complete hand
tlines for both fore and hindtracks are common. Field Voles usually run with their bodies close to the
ound, but scuff marks rarely occur. The tracks show in pairs and point slightly outwards with a stride of
ound 5–6cm (1.96–2.36in). Registration of the hind and foretracks does not often occur.

Common or Orkney Vole

British Distribution

COMMON OR ORKNEY VOLE
Body length: **7–13.5cm** (2.76–5.3in). *Tail length:* **2–4.5cm** (0.8–1.75in).

   Microtus arvalis is extremely similar to the Field Vole, but the yellow-brown fur is shorter and the ears are not as hairy. The underside of the Common Vole is pale grey. Only by careful examination of the dental structure can these two species be accurately separated.

   Common Voles prefer dry and short-stemmed grassland, whereas the Field Vole thrives equally well in wet meadows. Even where the two species share grassland habitats, the Common Vole is more numerous where the grass is shorter.

   Apart from Guernsey (Channel Islands) and the Orkney Islands, where it is the only species, this vole is not found in Britain, but occurs throughout most of Europe except the Mediterranean countries and Scandinavia.

   Common Voles are diligent burrowers, and because of this can survive in habitats with little ground cover. They breed from February to September, with up to 5 young in a litter and a life expectancy of just over a year. On Orkney, where they live on moors up to 200m (660ft) they are preyed upon by hen harriers.

90

European Distribution

Left hind track

Left fore track

ommon Vole (Order *Rodentia*)

imilar species: Possible confusion with Bank Vole (*Clethrionomys glareolus*, page 86) and Field Vole *Microtus agrestis*, page 88).

ield signs and clues: Grassland and fields bordering cultivated land are pock-marked with small holes –4cm (1.18–1.57in) in diameter and often suggest the presence of this species. A network of tunnels and ns criss-cross just beneath the ground surface, but often well-worn runways occur through the surface egetation and are immediately obvious. Some of these runways reach 6m (19.6ft.) long. Grass clippings redded by the vole frequently litter the runs and tunnels. Common Voles deposit their droppings in gular latrines, which are spaces along the tunnels or pathways free from vegetation. The droppings are reen or black cylindrical pellets, measuring 0.3–0.4cm (0.11–0.15in) long. Even when the ground is overed with snow Common Voles are active at ground level, gnawing bark from saplings beneath the snow vel. The areas of stripped bark become obvious when the snow thaws and provides a positive clue to the ole's presence.

As with all voles, the tracks of this species are difficult to find, but there are 5 digits on the hind feet d 4 on the forefeet, splayed out in a star-like arrangement. The tracks are similar to those of the Field ole, but are larger, measuring 1.8 x 1.2cm (0.7 x 0.4in). They normally run through their habitat, roducing a stride of 3.5–4.5cm (1.37–1.77in).

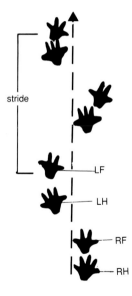

stride

LF

LH

RF

RH

Running gait

91

Northern Water Vole – melanistic or black form

NORTHERN WATER VOLE *Body length:* **12–23.5cm** (4.7–9.2in). *Tail length:* **5–14.5cm** (2–5.7in).

Arvicola terrestris is about the size of a Brown Rat and is sometimes confused with it, although the dark brown fur, rounded face, blunt nose and shorter tail should help positive identification. The Water Vole's fur is characteristically long and glossy, and hides the small furry ears. Completely black individuals occur in Scotland and in parts of Europe.

Unlike rats, Water Voles require clean, unpolluted water, such as lowland rivers, pond and lakes, where they feed on aquatic plants, found within a narrow ribbon of land near the waters edge. Their territories cover about 130m (425ft) of bankside, where they excavate a burrow system with some entrances below the water level. When they dive into the water, they make a distinctive 'plop' and use all four legs to paddle away.

This species is common in central and northern Europe, but is replaced by the Southwestern Water Vole in France and Iberia. A woven plant-stem nest is built above or below ground, where 4–6 young are born from March to October.

Similar species: The Brown Rat (*Rattus norvegicus*, page 80) and the Muskrat (*Ondatra zibethica*, page 94).

Field signs and clues: Water Voles excavate tunnels with entrances of 8cm (3.14in) at various levels along a river or canal bank. Immediately around these holes the vegetation is closely grazed, producing a 'feeding lawn' 15–99.8cm (6–39.3in) across. Runways 4–9cm (1.5–3.5in) across and within 1m (3.28ft) of the water's edge are easily observed through the bankside vegetation. Flattened platforms occur wherever Water Voles regularly enter and leave the water.

92

Northern Water Vole (Order *Rodentia*)

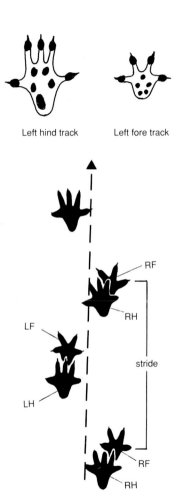

Left hind track   Left fore track

RF
RH
LF
LH

stride

RF
RH

Running gait showing partial registration

Elsewhere bare patches of soil, prominent stones or tussocks of vegetation are piled with chopped reeds, sedges and grass blades, ready for eating. These are the characteristic feeding stations of the Water Vole and the bitten vegetation shows the imprint of the two large incisors used for cutting. Whenever they grow close by, turnips and potatoes are damaged below ground by feeding Water Voles. The wilting surface foliage indicates the crop is being attacked by this rodent. They also gnaw the bark of ash and willow trees to a height of about 20cm (8in). It is chewed off in characteristic strips 0.5–1cm (0.19–0.39in) across with a distinct curve at one end. Most strips are left lying along the riverbank and clearly show teeth marks along their edges. Favourite feeding sites are also used as latrines, where the cylindrical droppings accumulate in large numbers. They are 1–1.2cm (0.39–0.47in) long with a diameter of 0.5cm (0.19in), smooth surfaced and are light green or khaki. The hind tracks measure 3 x 3.1cm (1.18 x 1.22in) with 5 digits and digital pads. A distinguishing feature is the elongated proximal pad, which shows clearly in the complete hand outline. Foretracks measure 1.8 x 2.3cm (0.7 x 0.9in) with 4 digits and digital pads. The short claws show well on all the tracks. Water Vole tracks are distinguished from rat tracks by the short heel on the hind feet and by the clear star shape of the foretracks. During the normal running gait the hind feet partially register over the foretracks with a stride of 6–10cm (2.4–4in). Whenever bounding, the tracks occur in groups of 4 with around 30cm (12in) between each group.

93

Muskrat swimming

No British Distribution

British Distribution

MUSKRAT *Body length:* **24–40cm** (9.4–15.7in). *Tail length:* **19–28cm** (7.4–11in).

Sometimes confused with the Beaver when swimming, *Ondatra zibethicus* is much smaller, with dark brown upper fur and paler undersides. The feet are not webbed, although the large hind feet bear thick bristles along the sides of the toes. Introduced into Europe from America in 1905 for its fur or musquash, many animals escaped, colonizing slow-flowing rivers, lakes and marshes, wherever the vegetation was dense. Apart from the British Isles, Iberia, Italy and Greece, the Muskrat is established throughout central and northern Europe, where it tunnels into banks and builds lodges in the middle of shallow, inland lakes.

Muskrats are active throughout the day, but especially early morning, and are territorial, marking their boundaries with musk from specialized glands. They can swim effectively, and although mainly vegetarian, can dive for mussels and even fish. Fox and mink are their main predators. Breeding occurs from March to September, with several litters a year, and up to 10 young per litter, although breeding is less prolific in northern Europe.

Similar species: The European Beaver (*Castor fiber*, page 62) and Coypu (*Myocastor coypus*, page 64) can cause confusion at a distance.

Field signs and clues: Cornfields bordering rivers and marshland are one of the best places to observe signs of the Muskrat. At dusk they feed on the corn, leaving stalks severed about 25cm (9.8in) from the ground. They also leave discarded mussel shells along riverbanks and the margins of reedbeds, having chewed through the edges of the shells to extract the flesh.

94   Muskrat runways and paths are about 20–30cm (8–12in) wide, and are easy to find in bank-side vegetation and across firm marshland. They are confirmed by the piles of droppings left at

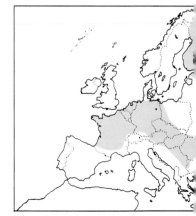
European Distribution

Muskrat (Order *Rodentia*)

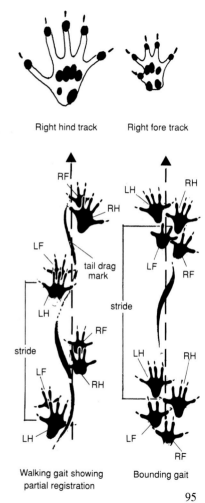

Right hind track   Right fore track

Walking gait showing   Bounding gait
partial registration

the beginning and end of each run. Alternatively, the droppings are deposited on raised platforms such as raised tufts, piles of bare earth, fallen tree trunks or large rocks projecting from the riverbank. They are similar to those of the Water Vole (*Arvicola terrestris*, page 92), but are larger, measuring up to 1.5cm (0.59in) long and 0.5cm (0.2in) wide. Resembling an olive stone, they vary in colour from green to black.

Both fore and hind feet leave characteristic star-shaped tracks bearing 5 digits and often revealing the complete hand outline. The hind tracks measure 6 x 6.5cm (2.4 x 2.6in) with distinct oval digital pads and long, narrow claws. The 4 interdigital pads are partially fused, whereas the 2 proximal pads are distinctly separate. Foretracks measure 3.5 x 3.5cm (1.4 x 1.4in) with small rounded digital pads, although the inside digit often fails to imprint in the track. There are 3 interdigital pads which barely fuse and 2 proximal pads which show clearly in the complete hand outlines in soft mud. During the walking gait the hind tracks partially register over the foretracks with a stride of about 10cm (4in) and an undulating tail drag mark is common. Moving at a bound, the tracks occur in groups of 4, with the hind feet ahead of the forefeet, and the tail drag showing distinctly between each group. During bounding movements the stride varies between 15–40cm (6–16in) depending on speed.

Muskrats also build noticeable lodges, but these are smaller and more fragile than beaver lodges and are constructed in shallow, open water.

95

The heavy bodied Brown Bear

BROWN BEAR *Body length:* **170–250cm** (66–98in).

Ursus arctos is instantly recognized by its size, muscular limbs and powerful neck. Its woolly fur is variably coloured from dark brown to creamy fawn, although usually it is a light yellow-brown.

Once widespread throughout Europe, they have been persecuted by man, and today only isolated populations occur in wild mountainous regions, coniferous forests and marshes of central and southern Europe. Other populations occur in European Russia and Scandinavia, but they became extinct in Britain by the 10th century and in Germany by 1836.

Brown bears are solitary except during the mating season between May and July, maintaining a 10–15km (6–9 mile) diameter territory. Mainly nocturnal, they are chiefly herbivorous, preferring wild fruits, fungi and roots but also eating rodents, amphibians and birds. Wild pigs, domestic cattle and deer are easily killed with a lethal swipe from the forelimbs. Generally they are not aggressive to man, frequently bounding off if approached, although unprovoked attacks are known.

Usually two small cubs are born in January or February and open their eyes after one month. They stay with their mother for most of the following year.

Similar species: Throughout its restricted European range, the Brown Bear cannot be confused with any other animal.

Field signs and clues: As one of the largest, strongest and most unpredictable of European carnivores, Brown Bears demand respect from the naturalist. They will defend themselves, their young and territory if they feel threatened, so knowledge of their signs and awareness of their presence is mainly to prevent an encounter rather than to actively locate them. Actual observations are difficult because of their almost inaccessible habitats. Feeding signs are the most obvious – large gaping pits in the soil indicate bears have been digging for rodents. Ragged,

No British Distribution

British Distribution

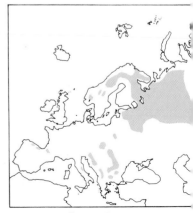

European Distribution

Right hind track   Left fore track

Brown Bear (Order *Carnivora*)

uprooted plants, with a few remaining berries are positive signs that the Brown Bear has been eating fruits and shoots. A shallow depression, covered with a loose mound of earth, leaves and branches, usually conceals a cache of a recent kill. It should be avoided because the bear will not be far away. This species also has favourite 'bear trees', where they scratch their bodies by rubbing against them. The bark of these trees is sometimes worn smooth and polished from rubbing over several seasons. Tufts of brown hair may occur around the base of such trees or be stuck behind areas of rough bark. Elsewhere Brown Bears like to bite into tree bark and sharpen their claws on the trunk, leaving 4 parallel marks 4–8cm (1.57–3.14in) long. These bark-shredded trees are instantly recognized by the tooth marks at the height of a man's head and claw slash marks almost twice as high.

    During the summer the bear builds a bed in a depression about 30.4cm (12in) deep, with a diameter of 1.22m (4.8ft), and lines it with dry leaves and pine needles. Winter dens are usually in caves or in holes dug beneath large tree root systems.

    Brown Bear tracks are enormous, the forefeet prints measuring 23–30 x 17cm (9–11 x 6.7in) and the hind feet 25–30 x 17cm (9.8–11 x 6.7in). All feet possess 5 extremely long claws which show clearly in the tracks, together with large pads. The normal gait is a walk with a stride of 80–100cm (31.5–40in) and each foot is turned slightly inwards. When trotting the trail changes so that the hind track is placed in front of the preceding fore-track.

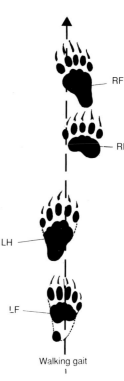

RF

RH

LH

LF

Walking gait

Wolf, showing powerful body

WOLF *Body length:* **110–140cm** (43–55in). *Tail length:* **30–40cm** (11–15in).

Canis lupus is similar to a large Alsatian, but is more powerfully built with broader head, thicker neck and larger teeth. The coarse, dense fur varies, depending upon season, territory and age, from light grey-brown to dark yellow-brown. The black-edged ears are always held erect, whereas the bushy tail droops.

The wolf became extinct in the British Isles in 1743, but isolated populations still occur in Italy and Spain and throughout Scandinavia, where they are protected. In eastern Europe, populations are healthier and it is still common in Russia. Throughout their range, wolves inhabit forests, mountains, tundra and steppe, usually hunting in packs by day over a wide range. Prey includes reindeer, elk, domestic livestock, birds and small rodents. Fruit is also eaten.

Mating occurs between January and March with 5–6 cubs born in a den, between rocks or in a cave. Blind at birth, the cubs open their eyes at 12 days and leave the den after 3 months, remaining as a family throughout the autumn.

No British Distributio

British Distribution

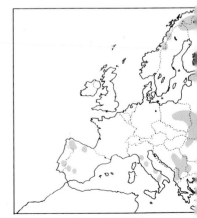

European Distribution

Wolf (Order *Carnivora*)

Similar species: Large domestic dogs may look wolf-like from a distance and the Jackal (*Canis aureus*), although smaller and slighter in build, can cause confusion wherever their ranges overlap.

Field signs and clues: Requiring a great deal of patience, the Wolf is one of the most difficult European mammals to observe, despite its presence being confirmed by obvious tracks. These are similar to those of domestic dogs, but the four digits are spaced wider apart and the spread between the two middle claws is significantly wider. Both fore and hind feet possess 4 digits and the well-developed claws show clearly in the tracks. The forefoot track is slightly larger than the hind foot, measuring 11 x 10cm (4.4 x 4in). Wolves rarely walk, but when they do the length of the stride is around 80–90cm (31.5–36in). The usual loping trot leaves a straight trail in mud or snow with a stride of around 120cm (48in) and the tracks arranged in pairs. Wolf droppings are characteristic, measuring 10–15cm (4–6in) long and 2–3cm (0.78–1.2in) in diameter and contain lots of hair and pieces of bone.

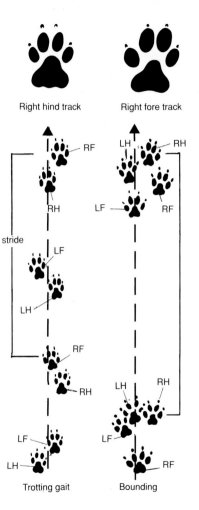

Right hind track   Right fore track

stride

RF
RH
LF
LH
RF
RH
LF
LH

Trotting gait

LH   RH
LF   RF
LH   RH
LF
RF

Bounding

Red Fox yawning

FOX *Body length:* **58–90cm** (22–35in). *Tail length:* **32–48cm** (12.5–18.8in).

With its bushy tail bearing a white tip, large ears and narrow muzzle, *Vulpes vulpes* is very distinctive. Extremely variable in colour, the coat is usually reddish-brown with lighter undersides and a silvery rump. The lower legs and back of the ears are black. The coat is at its best from October to January, because moulting occurs during the summer.

Foxes are ever wary, with a keen sense of smell and alert hearing. They are typically a woodland mammal, but are adaptable, colonizing farmland, uplands and increasingly suburbia. Dusk and night-time activity are the most common, but in undisturbed areas foxes roam during daylight, feeding on rodents, birds, beetles, fruits and even domestic refuse. Surplus food is usually cached. For several hours after sunset foxes utter high-pitched barks and yelps and the vixen has an eerie scream during the mating season from December to February. 4–9 cubs are born in spring and remain with their mother until the autumn, when they disperse. The Fox is widespread throughout Europe.

British Distribution

European Distribution

Fox (Order *Carnivora*)

Hind track   Fore track

Similar species: The Arctic Fox (*Alopex lagopus*, page 102) and Racoon-dog (*Nyctereutes procyonoides*).
Field signs and clues: Apart from the characteristic staccato bark, foxes also carry a strong musty odour which lingers on vegetation and reveals where the animal has recently passed. Red-brown hair and scratches around gate posts and rodent burrows indicate where digging has occurred, and the discarded remains of recent killings, including feathers, fur and bones are positive signs of fox. Food remains are often left outside the entrance to the earth. Long, tapering, greenish-brown or blue-brown droppings confirm the presence of foxes.

    Their tracks are common in mud along road verges, river margins and hedgerows, and although the Red Fox has 5 digits on the forefeet and four on each hind foot, all tracks only show 4 digits. The inner toe of the forefoot is positioned high up the paw and therefore leaves no impression. All prints are about 5 x 4.5cm (1.96 x 1.77in) and the two central digits generally point slightly outwards. The normal trotting gait is purposeful and straight with a stride of about 25cm (10in), but whenever the fox bounds, all feet are put down in a group of four and there is a 60cm (24in) distance between each group.

stride

RH
LH
RH

Walking gait

Fox dropping

Arctic Fox looking for prey

No British Distribution

British Distribution

ARCTIC FOX *Body length:* **50–85cm** (19.6–33.4in). *Tail length:* **28–55cm** (11–21.6in).

Alopex lagopus is much smaller than the Red Fox (*Vulpes vulpes*, page 100), with extremely thick fur to protect it against the cold. In winter the fur is pure white, but in summer it moults to grey brown on the head, upper body and outside of the legs. The belly is greyish-white. This nomadic species colonizes the coastal plains, tundra and mountain slopes above the tree line and is especially active at dusk, when it hunts for lemmings, voles and ground-nesting birds and their eggs. Territories are established in spring and mating occurs in March and April. Between 5 and 10 blind cubs are born in a subterranean den in May–June and are weaned within a month. Arctic Foxes mate for life and maintain contact by uttering characteristic 3–5-noted barks. They have become much bolder since man has entered their Arctic habitat and have learnt to enter settlements to steal food. They also plunder bars of soap from storehouses, which they bury near their dens! Apart from Polar Bears, they have few natural enemies and live for 12–14 years.

European Distribution

Arctic Fox (Order *Carnivora*)

Similar species: No other animal is similar within the range of the Arctic Fox.
Field signs and clues: The harsh barking cries of the adults first disclose their whereabouts, but the barks turn to yelping calls and howls during courtship. Their territories are marked with strong, scented urine, which is easily detected. The droppings are small for a member of the dog family, between 1–6cm (0.4–2.36in) long and not twisted like those of the Red Fox. When first deposited they are dark and although they may occur in small piles near the den, they are generally deposited randomly. A strong musty and urine odour accompanies the droppings and is a positive clue to the presence of this species.

Typically the Arctic Fox bounds or gallops through its habitat so that the hind feet are placed close to the footprints of the forefeet. The tracks are small, about 5.5 x 5cm (2.2 x 2in) and both fore and hind tracks usually show only 4 digits, but sometimes the fifth claw on the forefeet imprints in very soft ground or snow. Fur impressions are always revealed between the pad markings. During the walking gait, the stride measures 40cm (15.7in), increasing to 60–100cm (23.6–40in) when in full gallop. The tail leaves a drag mark in soft snow.

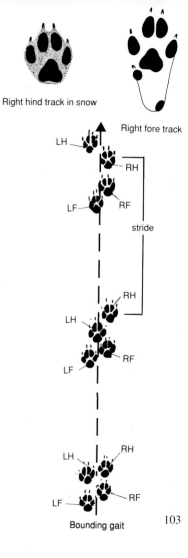

Right hind track in snow

Right fore track

LH

RH

LF

RF

stride

RH

LH

RF

LF

LH

RH

LF

RF

Bounding gait

103

Stoat in profile

British Distribution

STOAT *Body length:* **18–31cm** (7–12.2in). *Tail length:* **5.5–12.5cm** (2.1–4.9in).

Mustela erminea has reddish-brown upper parts with a creamy white belly. The tail has a diagnostic black tip and even those stoats in the northern part of their range, which turn white during winter, retain this feature.

Found throughout Europe, except Iceland and the Mediterranean regions, stoats are excellent swimmers and climbers, actively hunting through woods, scrubland, farmland and dense hedgerows. Generally solitary, families occur during the breeding season. The den is usually a rock crevice, a crack in a stone wall, or a disused rabbit burrow, and mating takes place in summer, with 5–12 kittens born the following spring. The young hunt and play as a family group, becoming independent after 10 weeks.

Stoats are constantly alert and are fierce predators, killing prey by biting into the neck. Rabbits, rodents and birds form the bulk of the diet, with males eating twice as much as females.

104

European Distribution

Left hind trail

Right fore track

Stoat (Order *Carnivora*)

Similar species: The Weasel (*Mustela nivalis*, page 106), American Mink (*Mustela vison*, page 108) European Mink (*Mustela lutreola*) and Polecat (*Mustela putorius*, page 110).

Field signs and clues: Any carcasses of reptiles, birds and small mammals such as hares or rabbits, with the rear of the skull bitten through, are typically the work of the Stoat. Because of its small size and light weight, tracks are only clear in very soft ground or snow. Each foot has 5 splayed digits and the claw marks usually show. The forefoot track is about 2 x 1.5cm (0.78 x 0.6in) and the hind foot 3.5 x 1.5cm (1.37 x 0.6in). Stoats generally jump or bound through their habitat so that the hind feet perfectly implant in the forefoot tracks or are placed very close, forming a group of 4 tracks with about 20cm (8in) between each group.

Stoat dropping

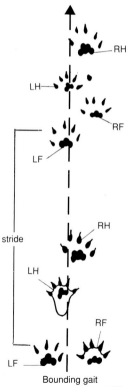

Bounding gait

Weasel with prey

WEASEL *Body length:* up to **22cm** (8.75in). *Tail length:* **7.5cm** (3in).

Mustela nivalis is Britain's smallest carnivore with brown upper parts and white flanks and belly. There are small brown patches on the throat, but the short brown tail does not have a black tip, neither does the Weasel turn white in winter.

It is common in most habitats, occupying territories of 4–8 hectares (10–20 acres) including parks, woodland and hillsides. Apart from Ireland and some off-shore islands, weasels are found throughout the British Isles and Europe, reaching the Mediterranean islands with man's assistance.

They are constantly active, moving rapidly, and often stand on their hind feet when they attempt to seize birds. Voles, mice, rats and rabbits are favourite prey and a weasel eats nearly 25 per cent of its body weight daily.

From April to May young weasels are born in a fur-lined nest, built in a crevice or hole. Second litters often occur in late summer, with independence reached at 12 weeks. Young weasels are able to breed in their first summer.

British Distribution

European Distribution

106

Weasel (Order *Carnivora*)

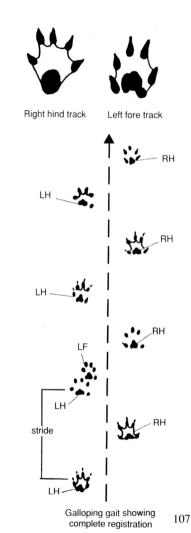

Right hind track   Left fore track

RH

LH

RH

LH

RH

LF

LH

stride

RH

LH

Galloping gait showing
complete registration

Similar species: The Stoat (*Mustela erminea*, page 104), American Mink (*M. vison*, page 108), European Mink (*M. lutreola*) and Polecat (*M. putorius*, page 110).
Field signs and clues: Weasels leave similar tracks in soft mud to the Stoat, but each impression is smaller, around 1.5–2 x 1cm (0.6–0.78 x 0.39in). During the normal bounding movement, the stride averages less than 30cm (11.8in) and this is the best way to distinguish a Weasel trail from that of the Stoat.

Feral American Mink with prey

British Distribution

AMERICAN MINK *Body length:* **30–47cm** (11.8–18.5in). *Tail length:* **13–23cm** (5–9in).

Mustela vison is a medium-sized member of the Weasel family which was introduced to Britain in the 1920s for breeding on commercial fur farms. Many escaped, and since 1930 feral populations have bred throughout Britain, eastern Europe, Scandinavia and the Soviet Union. The truly wild form has very dark brown fur, with white on the lower lip and chin and sometimes white patches between the forelegs. Other colour variations, including white and cream, are also found. Chiefly nocturnal, this species is largely aquatic, with similar habitats to the European Mink, where it feeds on fish, amphibians and crayfish, although small mammals form the bulk of its diet. Territories include a riverbank 1.5–4.5km (0.9–2.7 miles long) and it is regularly marked with foul-smelling droppings called spraints. Within the territory the mink has several dens, under an exposed tree-root system, inside a hollow tree or in an enlarged burrow. They are solitary animals outside of the breeding season and mating occurs from February to April, with 4–6 young born from May onwards.

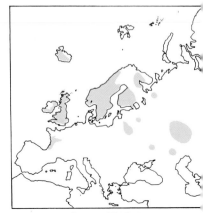
European Distribution

American Mink (Order *Carnivora*)

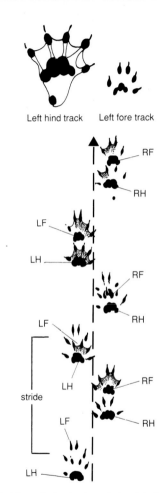

Left hind track   Left fore track

Ambling gait showing imperfect registration

Similar species: The European Mink (*Mustela lutreola*), Polecat (*M. putorius*, page 110), Stoat (*M. erminea*, page 104) and Weasel (*M. nivalis*, page 106).

Field signs and clues: Discarded prey carcasses left behind by American Mink are difficult to distinguish from those of a Stoat or Weasel, but they do prey more heavily on fish than most other members of this family. The cylindrical droppings are mucilaginous and contain bones, scales or fur, depending on the diet, and are 6–8cm (2.4–3.2in) long. They are similar to Otter and Polecat droppings.

The American Mink has 5 digits on all feet and the forefoot track measures 3 x 4cm (1.18 x 1.57in) whereas the hind foot is 4.5 x 3.5cm (1.77 x 1.37in). The digital pads and long claws are clearly marked in soft ground and the web between the digits frequently shows. During the arch-backed gallop the trail is almost perfectly registered with a stride of 30–40cm (12–16in), but the tracks become imperfectly registered when the mink ambles, forming groups of four imprints followed by a tail drag-mark if the mud is soft or covered with snow.

109

Polecat with prey

British Distribution

POLECAT *Body length:* **29–46cm** (11.4–18in). *Tail length:* **9–18cm** (3.5–7in).

Solitary by nature and active throughout the year, *Mustela putorius* has dark brown fur with white markings on the face, including muzzle and ears. The creamy-yellow underfur shows through the sparser, darker guard hairs, giving the animal a patchy appearance. Woodland, marshes, river banks and open farmland are popular habitats, but polecats are bold enough to visit outhouses and barns, and are adapting to live closer to man. In Britain they are confined to Wales and border counties, but occur throughout Europe except for the far north and south-east.

When alarmed, or marking territories, strong-smelling musk is released. They are mostly nocturnally active, but do hunt by day for rodents, rabbits, birds, reptiles and insects, using their keen sense of smell to locate prey. 5–10 young are born between March and June in a grass-lined nest, which is built close to the ground. They leave the nest after 2 months, but often remain in family groups until early autumn. Interbreeding with the domestic ferret is common.

110

European Distribution

Left hind track   Left fore track in snow

Polecat (Order *Carnivora*)

Similar species: The American Mink (*Mustela vison*, page 108), European Mink (*M. lutreola*), Stoat (*M. erminea*, page 104) and Weasel (*M. nivalis*, page 106).

Field signs and clues: The strong musky odour for which the polecat is famous is quickly detected in areas where the animal has recently been. Dusk is the time of greatest activity, when they hunt around rabbit warrens and river banks. In spring they hunt for breeding frogs, slaughtering hundreds by biting them through the spinal cord and storing them along the river margins. Such caches and remains of partially eaten frogs are positive signs of polecats in the locality.

    Their footprints are similar to those of Mink and in mud the forefoot measures 3.5 x 2.5–4cm (1.37 x 1–1.57in), depending on the splay of the 5 digits. However, in snow, where the animal supports itself on a flatter area of sole the hind foot track reaches up to 4.5cm (1.8in) long. A stride of 23cm (9in) between tracks is common when the polecat walks, but whenever they bound, the tracks are aggregated in groups of 4 with an average stride of 40–60cm (16–24in) between each group of tracks.

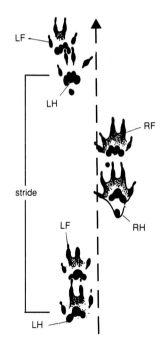

Walking gait   111

Pine Marten emerging from den

PINE MARTEN *Body length:* **36–56cm** (14.1–22in). *Tail length:* **17–28cm** (6.6–11in).

Martes martes is the most attractive member of the weasel family, with rich brown fur, bushy tail and conspicuous, variable, yellow-white throat patch. It is about the size of a domestic cat and, although generally silent can make screaming and purring noises, similar to a cat.

In the British Isles Pine Martens are localized in the remoter areas of North Wales, Highland Scotland and upland England, but they are widespread in Ireland. Apart from Iceland, Greece and the Iberian Peninsula, they are found right across Europe, inhabiting coniferous forests or mixed woodland, but also rocky hillsides. Outside the breeding season, martens are solitary and active during crepuscular hours. Despite being good swimmers and arboreally agile, most hunting is at ground level, where they catch rodents, hares and grouse. Squirrels and small birds are taken in the tree-tops and fruit forms part of the autumn diet. The den is usually in a rock crevice, with mating occurring in late summer and up to 3 martenettes born the following spring.

European Distribution

112

Pine Marten (Order *Carnivora*)

Similar species: The Beech Marten (*Martes foina*, page 114) and possibly Polecat (*Mustela putorius*, page 110) from a distance.

Field signs and clues: One of Europe's most elusive mammals and very difficult to see. Usually 10cm (4in) long, purple or mauve droppings, containing hair, feathers and bones, are seen first. They are deposited at regular intervals along forest tracks, on bare soil, prominent rocks or flat stones. Occasionally the droppings are left in the fork of a tree or mound, which the Pine Marten uses as a vantage point to survey the surrounding habitat.

The trail resembles that of a fox, but often stops at the base of a tree, where the marten has recently climbed. All feet have 5 digits, with sharp claws, but the prints often only reveal 4 digits and a large, multi-lobed central pad. Each track measures about 4.5 x 4cm (1.77 x 1.57in), but in snow the prints can be twice as large. During normal walking the tracks are randomly placed with a stride of around 50cm (20in), but when bounding the feet touch the ground in groups of two, with a stride of 60–90cm (24–36in) between each pair.

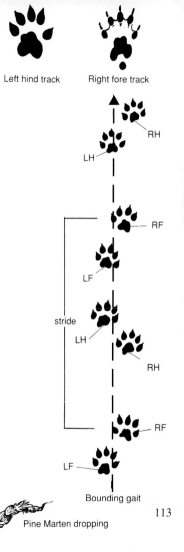

Left hind track

Right fore track

RH

LH

RF

LF

stride

LH

RH

RF

LF

Bounding gait

Pine Marten dropping

Beech or Stone Marten

No British Distribution

British Distribution

BEECH MARTEN *Body length:* **42–48cm** (16.5–18.8in). *Tail length:* **23–26cm** (9–10in).

Martes foina is a cat-sized animal similar to the Pine Marten but with bulkier body and shorter legs. The fur is pale brown, but lighter on the chin and triangular-shaped head. A white throat patch is usually obvious, although in the Cretan specimens is sometimes totally absent. The ears are short and pale brown with white edges and the eyes are dark brown.

Beech Martens inhabit open rocky ground, ravines, quarries and forests, although they frequently visit urban areas, living inside buildings, where they damage wiring. They lack a 'fixed habitat' and require spacious territories, travelling up to 10km (6.2 miles) a night in search of food, which includes fruit, small birds, mammals and insects. Domestic refuse is scavenged in urban areas. Except during the mating season, Beech Martens are nocturnal, rarely leaving their dens before twilight. Mating occurs in July and August, but with delayed implantation the 3–5 martenettes are born the following spring. Absent from the British Isles and Scandinavia, Beech Martens occur throughout Europe.

European Distribution

Beech Marten (Order *Carnivora*)

Left hind track   Right fore track

Similar species: The Pine Marten (*Martes martes*, page 112) and Polecat (*Mustela putorius*, page 110) from a distance.

Field signs and clues: Beech Martens regularly build their nests close to man, in old straw barns and outbuildings. Once the nest is discovered, sightings of the animal are likely, especially at dusk. They can be attracted to bait by placing raw eggs and fruit regularly in the same place.

Beech Martens sometimes deposit their droppings at random, but prefer to use a regular latrine such as the top of a particular haystack or corner of a farm building. This provides one of the most positive signs for Beech Marten.

In most respects the tracks and trails resemble those of the Pine Marten, but are smaller, yet more distinct. Five digits occur on all feet and the fore feet track measures 3.5 x 3.2cm (1.37 x 1.25in), whereas those of the hind feet are 4 x 3cm (1.57 x 1.18in). The walking stride measures 30cm (12in), extending to 40–60cm (16–24in) during the typical bounding gait.

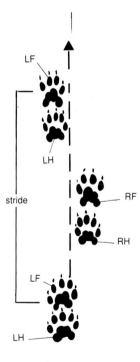

Walking gait

Otter on riverbank

British Distribution

European Distribution

OTTER *Body length:* **53–100cm** (20–39in). *Tail length:* **28–55cm** (11–21in).

Few people ever see *Lutra lutra* in the wild because they are elusive, mainly nocturnal animals. They are easily recognized, however, by their light brown fur, white bib, streamlined body and long, tapering tail. The eyes, nostrils and small ears are positioned well on top of the head to assist surface swimming and the broad, flattened head distinguishes it from mink. All four feet are webbed, providing a distinctive track in soft mud.

Undisturbed rivers, streams, marshes and estuaries are the favoured habitats, but sea lochs and remote coastlines are inhabited in Scotland. Pollution and hunting have resulted in a rapid decline in otters, with Scotland and Ireland remaining their strongholds in the British Isles. In Europe, where its distribution is widespread, populations are similarly dwindling. Otters are intelligent, inquisitive animals, thoroughly investigating their environment and feeding mostly on fish, amphibians, aquatic birds and rodents. Their holt is usually under tree roots, where 2–3 cubs are born from February to April and remain with their mother for about a year.

Similar species: The Coypu (*Myocastor coypus*, page 64) and Muskrat (*Ondatra zibethica*, page 94).
Field signs and clues: Dusk and early morning are the best times for observing this wary species. They are extremely playful and create 'otter slides' on river banks. These are long troughs of soft, smooth mud leading into the river or compressed runs in snow, down which otters slide straight into the water. Distinct runways are formed through bankside vegetation and along the muddy

116

Otter (Order *Carnivora*)

river margins. Since otters use regular routes, these are always kept well worn if the area is colonized. Otter droppings or spraints are deposited on stones, tufts of vegetation, tree trunks and projecting mud banks along the runway. They are green or black and glutinous with fish scales, fins and bones clearly visible. Otters also groom themselves fastidiously, rolling in grass and vegetation beside the river and leaving familiar flattened areas.

They are generally silent animals, but communicate with each other down-river by a piercing whistle. When nervous they utter deep purring growls and guttural moaning sounds.

Otters have 5 digits on each foot, joined by a web, but complete imprints only occur in very soft ground. The forefoot track is 6.5 x 6cm (2.55 x 2.3in) and almost circular, whereas the hind foot is 8.5 x 6cm (3.34 x 2.36in), and both have multi-lobed pads. The walking trail has a stride of 35cm (13.7in) with body and tail-drag markings, but often otters bound, leaving 4 precisely grouped tracks with 80–100cm (32–40in) between each group.

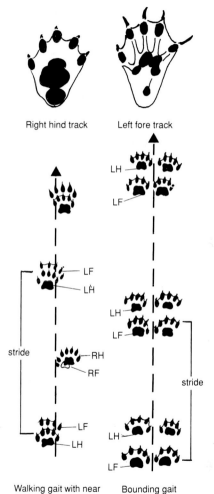

Right hind track

Left fore track

stride

LF
LH

RH
RF

LF
LH

Walking gait with near perfect registration

LH
LF

LH
LF

stride

LH
LF

Bounding gait

117

Badger cubs

BADGER *Body length:* **67–90cm** (26–35in). *Tail length:* **11–20cm** (4.3–7.8in).

Despite being mainly nocturnal, the heavily built *Meles meles*, with its grey-black fur, black and white striped head and powerful, long clawed front legs is one of the best-known European mammals.

Provided the soil is light and easy to dig, Badgers colonize any habitat ranging from deciduous woodland to farmland and scrubland. Railway embankments and suburban gardens are also frequented in Britain. Apart from some Mediterranean islands and the extreme north, Badgers are widespread in Europe. In the British Isles they occur everywhere except a few offshore islands.

Large sets provide shelter for family groups, each having several entrances leading into subterranean tunnels and chambers. Sleeping chambers are lined with dry straw and grass bedding, which is replaced regularly with clean material. During their nocturnal forages, Badgers amble clumsily along well-worn tracks eating worms, insects, slugs, amphibians and small mammals. Plants and wild fruits are eaten more during the autumn. 1–5 cubs are born from January to March and remain with the sow for their first year.

Similar species: The Badger cannot really be confused with any other European species.
Field signs and clues: Badgers use regular pathways which become well trodden into the grass and undergrowth and are immediately obvious. Where they pass under barbed wire fences, or close to brambles and twigs, tufts of grey and white hairs often become snagged. Fence posts and

118

Badger (Order *Carnivora*)

Left hind track   Right fore track

old tree trunks are regularly used for sharpening claws, which leave deep, parallel scour marks. These claws are also used to break into bees' and wasps' nests for the honey and any discarded pieces of honeycomb are usually a positive sign of a working Badger.

    Badgers are clean animals and deposit their dog-like droppings in small hollows or latrines, 5–10cm (2–4in) deep and about 20cm (8in) in diameter. Latrines are always dug some distance from the set, which is instantly recognized by its large tunnel entrance and surrounding mounds of excavated earth, largely devoid of vegetation. Badgers can often be heard at night without seeing them, because they move clumsily and noisily through the undergrowth, uttering frequent grunts.

    Their tracks with 5 long claws on each foot are easy to recognize with the forefoot measuring 6 x 5.5cm (2.36 x 2.16in) and the hind foot 6 x 5cm (2.36 x 2in). The claws are shorter on the hind feet. The normal gait is a walk with the hind feet registering in the tracks made by the forefeet. All tracks turn slightly inwards and the stride measures about 50cm (20in). When scared or crossing open ground rapidly, the Badger gallops, grouping all four tracks together with about 40cm (16in) between each group.

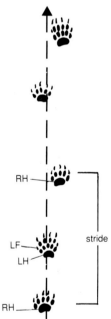

RH

LF
LH

RH

stride

Walking gait showing registration

Badger dropping

119

Feline, or Small-spotted Genet

No British Distribution

British Distribution

GENET *Body length:* **47–60cm** (18.5–23.6in). *Tail length:* **40–51cm** (15.7–20in).

Genetta genetta belongs to the mongoose family, but has the shape of a weasel and the movements of a cat. The pointed muzzle is more fox-like than cat-like, but the retractile claws and delicate paws are similar to those of a cat. Solitary and nocturnal by nature, the Genet's body fur is silver-grey, attractively marked with brown or black streaks and spots. The head is generally paler, but with darker cheeks and the disproportionately long tail shows light and dark bands.

Genets are agile and dexterous, climbing skilfully along branches and intensely scrutinizing their habitat, which includes woodlands, scrubland and rock slopes up to 2000m (6500ft), where they build a den in hollow trees and rock crevices. They hunt by stealth preying on small mammals, birds, reptiles and insects, but fruit is also eaten. The litter of 1–3 kittens is born in spring. Its range is south-west Europe, including Iberia, the Balearic Islands and most of France, where it is declining. Genets are absent from the British Isles.

European Distribution

Left hind track

Left fore track showing typical
incomplete outline

Genet (Order *Carnivora*)

Similar species: The Wild Cat (*Felis silvestris*, page 124)

Field signs and clues: Apart from when they are revealed at night in car headlights, Genets are rarely seen because of their secretive nature. Living mostly in trees or rocky areas they rarely leave footprints, but each foot has 5 digits with semi-retractile claws, although only 4 are revealed in the tracks. The forefoot tracks measure 3 x 2.5cm (1.18 x 1in) and those of the hind feet 3 x 3cm (1.18 x 1.18in) and resemble those of a domestic cat. Claw marks are left behind on tree trunks and fence posts, but are easily confused with those of Wild Cat, Pine Marten (*Martes martes*, page 112) and Beech Marten (*M. foina*, page 114). The black droppings are the most positive sign of Genets, since they are extremely large, measuring 10–24cm (4–9.6in) long and always forming a diagnostic horseshoe shape. They are deposited on a rocky shelf or fork of a tree, overlooking the animals' territory. Whenever Genets are disturbed, they utter high-pitched hisses and squeals in an attempt to frighten off the intruder.

Genet dropping

Female Lynx with cub

No British Distribution

British Distribution

LYNX *Body length:* **80–130cm** (31–51in). *Tail length:* **11–25cm** (4.3–10in).

Felis lynx resembles a long-legged, short-tailed tabby cat, but its ears and cheeks bear tufts. Its body fur is yellow-brown, with darker spots on the legs and lower body. The tail has a black tip.

Solitary by nature, except during the mating season, the Lynx is nocturnal, inhabiting coniferous forests, ravines and scrubland from 700–1100 m (2296–3610ft) above sea level. Like the domestic tom-cat, the Lynx marks its territory with urine and claw marks on tree trunks. Just before nightfall, lynxes begin hunting, locating their prey by sight and sound. Initially employing great stealth, the final attack is explosive, with the kill being made by a bite to the throat. Hares, small deer, rodents and gamebirds are the main prey. Mating occurs in March and April with 1–4 kittens born during May and June in a den amongst boulders or in a hollow tree. The Lynx is rare, but strict protection has caused an expansion of its range in eastern Europe, Scandinavia and Spain. They have been reintroduced to Switzerland.

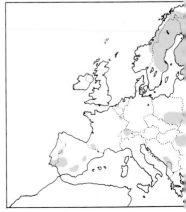

European Distribution

Lynx (Order *Carnivora*)

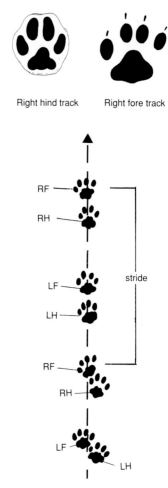

Right hind track   Right fore track

RF

RH

stride

LF

LH

RF

RH

LF

LH

Walking gait

Similar species: Any confusion is likely to be with the Wild Cat (*Felix silvestris*, page 124).

Field signs and clues: Their nocturnal behaviour makes the Lynx difficult to see, but their tracks, similar to Wild Cats, only larger, are distinctive. The forefoot track is around 6.5 x 5.5cm (2.55 x 2.16in) and the hind foot, 7.5cm x 6cm (2.95 x 2.36in) but the claw marks rarely show except in snow. On soft mud, fur markings occur between the pad impressions. Lynx normally walk so that the tracks appear in single file, because each hind foot perfectly registers in the track of the forefoot in a stride ranging between 40–80cm (16–32in). During a gallop the stride increases to around 150cm (60in). Like the Badger (*Meles meles*, page 118) the Lynx uses latrines or regular places to deposit droppings, which are fox-like in appearance and measure 25 x 3cm (9.8x1.18in).

Wild Cat showing aggression

WILD CAT *Body length:* **48–90cm** (18.8–36in). *Tail length:* **20–30cm** (8–12in).

    Similar to a large domestic cat, *Felis silvestris* has a characteristic bushy, dark ringed tail, with rounded black tip and grey-black stripes on yellow-grey body fur.

    They are most numerous in coniferous woodland and scrubland, and whereas Wild Cats used to be confined in Britain to Highland Scotland, they are spreading south into northern England, aided by increased afforestation. Central and southern Europe support increasing populations, although everywhere they are interbreeding with feral cats and weakening the pure strain.

    Chiefly nocturnal and solitary, these cats are agile climbers and good swimmers, but prefer to hunt rodents, rabbits, birds and amphibians on the ground, using a stalk and pounce technique. Dens are concealed amongst rocks or under fallen trees, wherever a good view of the surrounding territory is possible. 3–5 kittens are born in May and emerge from the den at 5 weeks old. Second litters sometimes occur in August with kittens becoming independent in autumn. Males are slightly larger than females.

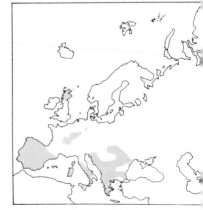
European Distribution

124

Wild Cat (Order *Carnivora*)

Similar species: The Lynx (*Felis lynx*, page 122) can cause misidentification from a distance.
Field signs and clues: Occasionally the remains of the cats' prey such as hare carcasses are found, or the dark grey-green 20cm (8in) droppings, which are twisted with tapering ends. Dusk is the best time to see glimpses of hunting Wild Cats, but they are very secretive. Scratching posts, which are normally old tree trunks, reveal claw marks. Whenever they climb favourite trees they also leave scratch marks behind, as a positive sign of habitat colonization. Although the forefeet of the cat have a fifth digit, it is placed so high that tracks in soft mud and snow only reveal four digits around a 3-lobed pad. The retractile claws rarely show in the track. The prints are almost circular, about 6 x 5cm (2.36 x 2in). The hind feet only have 4 digits.

When galloping the fore and hind feet tracks partially overlap and the stride is around 60cm (24in), but if walking, the Wild Cats' tracks do not overlap, with the hind foot being placed in front of the track made by the forefoot and a stride of 32cm (12.5in).

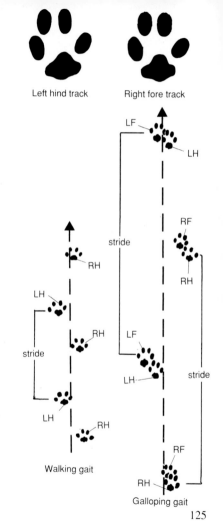

Left hind track   Right fore track

Walking gait

Galloping gait

125

Common Seal pup asleep

COMMON SEAL *Body length:* **170cm** (67in).

Phoca vitulina is the smallest seal found in British waters, recognized by its grey, mottled body, small head, short muzzle with concave profile and V-shaped nostrils when viewed head-on.

Shallow, sheltered, coastal water is the favourite habitat, especially estuaries and bays, where they feed on fish, molluscs and crustaceans. Each dive lasts for 5 to 10 minutes, but they can remain submerged for up to 30 minutes. At low tide this seal hauls itself up on to exposed rocks and sand-banks, where they can form large groups, although they dislike disturbance caused by humans seeking recreation in similar habitats. Breeding and non-breeding colonies occur throughout the eastern Atlantic with the European populations extending from the North Sea south to the Baltic. Forty per cent of this population are found in Britain and since 1987 many thousands have died from a mystery virus related to canine distemper. Increased pollution of the North Sea has lowered the resistance of the seals to disease and it will be many years before the European population of Common Seal recovers.

British Distribution

European Distribution

Common Seal (Order *Pinnipedia*)

Similar species: Despite being much larger and a different colour, the Grey Seal (*Halichoerus grypus*, page 128) might be confusing at a distance.

Field signs and clues: The feeding behaviour is similar to that of the Grey Seal, so no signs are left behind for the observer. They are generally silent mammals, but occasionally utter plaintive barks. In most respects the track resembles a smaller version of the Grey Seal. Five digits with sharp claws occur on both front flippers and although the tracks vary with the age of the seal, they are about 17 x 13cm (6.7 x 5.1in). The flippers form paired tracks either side of a wide body drag-mark and the distance between each pair of tracks, or stride, varies with speed of movement and animal size, but is normally over 30cm (12in).

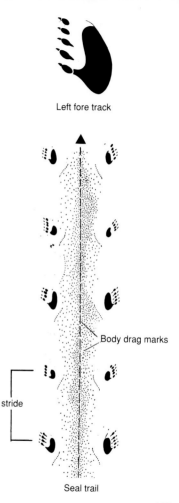

Left fore track

Body drag marks

stride

Seal trail

127

Grey Seal suckling pup

GREY SEAL *Body length:* up to **228cm** (90in).

Halichoerus grypus is variably marked, but the bull is dark grey with brown-grey blotches, becoming almost black when wet. The head is long and flattened on the top and there are thick rolls of blubber around the neck. Cows are paler, especially when dry, but have darker blotches, and are nowhere near as solidly built as the bulls. At birth, the single pup is covered in a creamy-white coat, which is shed after 2–3 weeks.

Colonies exist around the Scandinavian and northern European coasts, but 70 per cent of the world population live in British waters. They are completely marine, mainly feeding on large fish, but coming ashore to rocky islands and undisturbed beaches to breed in autumn. Although in 1988 the world population was estimated to be around 130,000, Grey Seals have been affected by seal distemper virus and colonies are dying in the North Sea, Scandinavia and the Orkneys and Hebrides, where Britain's largest population occurs. This seal is extremely vocal, uttering barking, moaning and hissing noises in the water and on land.

British Distribution

European Distribution

Grey Seal (Order *Pinnipedia*)

Similar species: The smaller Common Seal (*Phoca vitulina*, page 126) is the only other species which might be confused with the Grey Seal within its range. Other seals are mostly confined to Arctic waters.
Field signs and clues: Since the Grey Seal eats its prey in the water, there are no feeding signs or droppings left for the naturalist to find. In summer they form herds and spend hours basking on exposed rocks and sand banks and uttering a variety of prolonged trisyllabic, penetrating cries. Hoots and belching barks are the most familiar sounds, with the mature individuals giving the deepest notes and the younger seals making the barking calls.

Whenever Grey Seals come ashore on sand or soft mud, their tracks are unmistakable. The front flippers have 5 digits with well-developed claws which show clearly in the track, comprising a large palm area. The size of the track varies considerably with age and sex, but in adults measures at least 20 x 16cm (8 x 3.2in). The digital pad and claw marks lie in a line parallel to the direction of the seal's movement. When moving slowly up the beach, Grey Seals barely lift their body, but drag it over the surface by their forelimbs. The trail therefore shows a broad drag-mark of the body between the tracks, which occur in widely spaced, opposite pairs. The tail flippers do not leave tracks unless the seal takes off in panic, when they are used to provide rapid forward movement.

Grey Seal tracks and trails
resemble those
of Common Seal, but
are typically larger

129

Walrus on rocks showing hairy muzzle

No British Distribution

British Distribution

WALRUS

Body length: males up to **448.3cm** (176.5in); females up to **298cm** (117.5in).

With its wrinkled, virtually hairless skin and huge tusks, *Odobenus rosmarus* is unmistakable. The tusks are really elongated, upper jaw canine teeth and grow continuously throughout life, reaching 1m (3.28ft) in males. Young walrus possess a thin covering of pink-red body hair, which decreases with age, whereas the thickness of the skin increases with age. The Atlantic Walrus is found from north-eastern Canada, east to Greenland and is rare in European waters, visiting Svalbard and Novaya Zemlya. Occasionally individuals visit the North Sea and waters around the British Isles.

Living in areas of shallow water, they regularly haul themselves on to rocks or sea ice, forming herds. Walrus feed on molluscs, crustaceans and fish mostly dug up from the sea bed with the tusks. The facial whiskers which form a moustache of coarse but flexible hairs pass the food to the mouth, where the flesh is sucked from the prey. Females breed at 5 years old, with pups born during April and May and remaining dependent on parental milk for the first year. Their only natural enemies are polar bears and killer whales and they live for over 30 years.

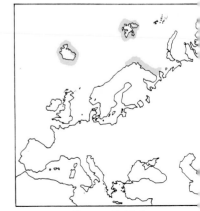

European Distribution

Walrus silhouette
– characteristic from a distance

Basking Walrus (Order *Pinnepidia*)

Similar species: The Walrus cannot be confused with any other species within its limited range.
Field signs and clues: Walrus spend more time out of the water than members of the seal family, but dive rapidly if they scent human presence and are difficult to approach closely. The most positive sign is their bellow, which can be heard up to 1.6km (1 mile) away. They rarely come ashore on to a substrate which reveals tracks, preferring rocky beaches and ledges or pack ice.

Field signs and clues: Walrus spend more time out of the water than members of the seal family, but dive rapidly if they scent human presence and are difficult to approach closely. During deep dives, blood goes from the skin to the internal organs, leaving the skin pale. After surfacing, the heartbeat is unusually rapid at first and the skin resumes its pink-brown colour as the Walrus basks. The most positive sign is their bellow, which can be heard up to 1.6km (1 mile) away. They rarely come ashore on to a substrate which reveals tracks, preferring rocky beaches and ledges or pack ice.

131

Dartmoor Pony

British Distribution

HORSE

During the end of the last Ice Age wild horses and Tarpans (*Equus ferus*) roamed the desolate plains of Europe. Climatic and vegetative changes as the ice retreated caused these animals to naturally decline, with the last truly wild horse being killed by man during the 1800s. Domesticated horses (*Equus caballus*) have been bred for over 5000 years, and throughout Europe, semi-wild or feral horses roam in remote areas. In Poland, wild ponies resulting from crossing wild and domestic horses survive in forest reserves and the Hucul of the Carpathians originates from the Wild Tarpan. Several breeds of primitive, semi-wild ponies are found in Britain, including the New Forest, Welsh Uplands, the Lake District, the Shetlands, Dartmoor and Exmoor. Exmoor ponies have been living wild since about 60,000 BC and although small (up to 12.3 hands/130cm high at the withers), they are extremely strong and hardy. New Forest Ponies have roamed freely since Saxon times and occur in every colour except skewbald and piebald. Living in small herds with a dominating stallion, wild ponies wander over large areas, browsing vegetation and breeding from March to November, according to weather conditions.

132

European Distribution

New Forest Pony (Order *Perissodactyla*)

Horse track

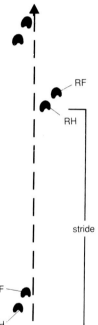

RF

RH

stride

LF

LH

RF

RH

Walking gait

Similar species: Cannot be confused with any other European animal.

Field signs and clues: Because the diet of the Horse is mainly grass and low-growing herbage, the droppings are the first obvious sign of the animal being nearby. They vary in size, but are generally large and cylindrical with a diameter of 5–7cm (2–2.75in). They are either dark brown or yellow-green in colour with distinct coarse remains of undigested plant tissue such as grass stems. Feral horses use traditional latrine sites some distance away from their main feeding areas. When communicating with each other, feral ponies utter a variety of whinnying calls which carry considerable distances. These familiar sounds are often heard before the animals are seen.

The large, almost circular track is quickly recognized, but varies in size according to age and breed. Since feral herds are unshod, the tracks are blunt and rounded at the front with almost flat sides. There is a deep, characteristic notch in the back. Small ponies form tracks measuring about 12 x 12cm (4.8 x 4.8in).

The gait of a horse varies considerably from walking, trotting, cantering and galloping. During a walk the tracks appear in groups of two, whereas during a gallop, the fore and hind tracks often partially register.

133

Wild Boar or Pig

No British Distribution

British Distribution

WILD BOAR *Body length:* **185cm** (72.8in). *Tail length:* **15–20cm** (5.9–7.8in).

With its hefty, compact body, large head and short, thin legs, *Sus scrofa* is the ancestor of the domestic pig, but its snout is elongated and its coat is coarse, dark and bristly and is always thicker in winter than in summer. The boar's canine teeth continually grow, producing short tusks. Deciduous woodland is the favoured habitat, but wild pigs venture into secluded agricultural land, causing serious damage to root crops. They are omnivorous, preferring to feed on acorns, beech mast, roots and plants, but also eating earthworms, insects, small rodents and even carrion.

Apart from November to February, when rutting usually takes place, the boars are solitary and mainly nocturnal. Females form small family groups with their young from successive litters. The young have distinctive chestnut and yellow-brown longitudinal stripes down their flanks, which disappear as they mature. Females alert their young to danger by uttering short grunts, but apart from various muffled calls, this species is silent. Extinct in Britain since the 17th century, wild pigs occur throughout southern and central Europe with reintroductions in Sweden and Norway.

134

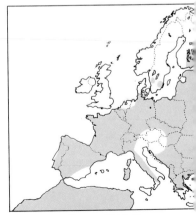

European Distribution

Wild Boar (Order *Artiodactyla*)

Right fore track

Similar species: This animal can only be confused with domestic pigs grazing as semi-feral herds.
Field signs and clues: Wild Boar enjoy wallowing in shallow depressions which they hollow out in soft mud with their snouts and forelegs. Once filled with rain water and urine, the wallow pit is trampled around and rolled in by the adult pigs and is a regular sign of an area being colonized. A nearby tree is often used for back and flank scratching and tufts of dark hairs lodged in the bark are positive clues. Large areas of pasture, arable land and woods are damaged by the 'rooting' behaviour of feeding Wild Boar. They create numerous muddy impressions by trampling and overturning earth in their search for roots, bulbs and insect larvae. This is one of the most regular signs of Wild Boar. The large, cloven-hoof track of this species is quite characteristic because the vestigial second and fifth digits or dew claws, always leave clear impressions. A diagnostic feature is that Wild Boar tracks are always broadest across the dew claw area. Tracks vary with age and sex, but are generally 12cm (4.8in) long to the back of the dew claws and 7cm (2.8in) across them. The cleaves or hooves are broad and rounded. During walking and trotting gaits, each track is turned slightly outwards and the hind feet almost imprint or register exactly in the forefeet tracks with a stride of about 40cm (15.7in).

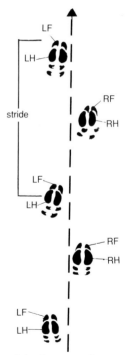

Trotting gait showing near perfect registration

135

Mouflon – a species of wild sheep

No British Distribution

British Distribution

MOUFLON *Body length:* **110–130cm** (43.3–51in). *Tail length:* **3.5–6cm** (1.3–2.3in).

Ovis musimon is a small wild sheep with its wool concealed under a coat of straight body hair. Rams are characteristically reddish-brown on the upper body with black patches on the neck and upper legs. A white 'saddle' marking adorns both flanks and the rump, muzzle and lower legs are also white. Fully grown rams possess large, curved, wrinkled horns. Native to Cyprus, Corsica and Sardinia, the Mouflon has been introduced to central and southern Europe. Ewes show no flank patches and those on Corsica grow small horns, whereas Sardinian ewes are hornless.

Steep, mountainous, wooded slopes are the main habitat with the sheep feeding on vegetation, especially at night. They are gregarious, but males form separate flocks to the females and young and all Mouflons hide in cover during daylight, yet are swift and agile once disturbed. During the winter rut, the rams engage in fierce battles, head-butting each other to gain supremacy. During April and May, 1–2 lambs are born, with a life expectancy of 12 years.

European Distribution

136

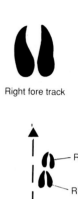

Right fore track

Mouflon (Order *Artiodactyla*)

Similar species: The Chamois (*Rupicapra rupicapra*, page 140), Alpine Ibex (*Capra ibex*, page 138) and domestic sheep cause confusion.

Field signs and clues: Mouflon are wary animals and difficult to approach. Signs of their presence include gnawed trees, especially during winter. Their lower incisor teeth leave oblique grooves in the soft wood beneath the outer bark, whereas similar tooth marks of deer run vertically. The droppings are spherical with a diameter of about 1cm (0.4in) and are deposited in small groups. They can easily be confused with the droppings of domestic sheep and even Roe Deer (*Capreolus capreolus*, page 154).

It is virtually impossible to distinguish the tracks of Mouflon from feral sheep, which colonize the same habitat. In a mature ram, the tracks are about 6 x 4.5cm (2.36 x 1.78in) and only slightly smaller in a ewe. Even at slow speeds, the cleaves obviously splay and the tips imprint deeply, whereas the heels are characteristically rounded. Their outer walls are distinctly convex. The dew claws are set a long way back and rarely show except when the sheep moves rapidly across deep snow.

Walking or trotting are the normal gaits with hind-foot and forefoot registration being almost perfect during a walk, when the stride is about 90cm (36in). The tracks occur in groups of four during a gallop with up to 150cm (60in) between each group.

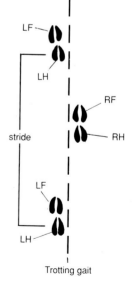

Trotting gait

137

Alpine Ibex are sure-footed goats

No British Distribution

British Distribution

ALPINE IBEX *Body length:* **130–150cm** (51–59 in). *Tail length:* **12–15cm** (4.7–5.9in).

Strictly protected throughout Europe, *Capra ibex* is a robust goat of high-altitude, mountainous slopes, well above the tree line. They are extremely agile, negotiating the most precipitous terrain, with their brown and brownish-grey bodies perfectly camouflaging them against the rocks. The males, which are more nomadic and occupy higher ground than females, possess long, backwardly curved horns with ridges on the front surface. Females have much smaller horns and form small flocks with their young lower down the slopes, occupying territories of around 1 sq. km (0.4 sq. mile). Diurnally active, but elusive, Alpine Ibex prefer to feed on shrubs, grasses and sedges during late afternoon and early evening. Lichens become important for survival during the winter.

During December and January, the males disregard their solitary lifestyle and actively rut. The kids are born during May and June and although a single kid is the norm, occasionally twins are born. Alpine Ibex were once only found in Italy's Gran Paradiso National Park, but have been introduced to the Swiss and Austrian Alps and Yugoslavia.

European Distribution

Alpine Ibex (Order *Artiodactyla*)

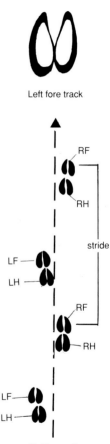

Left fore track

stride

Trotting gait

Similar species: The Chamois (*Rupicapra rupicapra*, page 140), Mouflon (*Ovis musimon*, page 136) and domestic goats can be confusing.

Field signs and clues: This species is not timid and is regularly observed. Their droppings are virtually spherical with slightly flattened ends and about 1cm (0.4in) long and deposited in groups. They closely resemble droppings of feral goats.

Because of its rocky habitat, the Alpine Ibex leaves few tracks behind, but they are similar to those of domestic goats and measure 7.5cm x 5cm (3 x 2in). The cleaves are unevenly shaped, and whereas they touch at the back, they splay towards the front. The hind contact of the cleaves is a diagnostic feature of the tracks and the dew claws do not show themselves.

During a trotting gait, the parallel tracks reveal slight registration between fore and hind feet with a stride of about 90cm (36in). Juvenile Alpine Ibex show a more complete track registration.

Chamois suckling kid

British Distribution

CHAMOIS *Body length:* **110–130cm** (43–51in).

The bold black and white head markings and erect, button-hook horns make *Rupicapra rupicapra* unmistakable, even over long distances. During summer the coat is reddish brown, with dark black-brown legs and dark dorsal stripe. Following an autumn moult, the entire coat becomes thicker and dark brown. Generally living at lower altitudes than the Ibex, Chamois are extremely agile, grazing vegetation from precipitous ledges in the Alps and Pyrenees, north to the Tatras. Elsewhere in Europe they have been introduced.

In spring and autumn, the tree line is the preferred altitude, where they even browse conifers, but in summer chamois move higher, descending again in winter to forests as low as 800m (2624ft). Gregarious by nature, females and young form groups of up to 100 animals, with the more solitary male joining the females during the rutting season, which begins in October. During the rut, males mark their territories with scent glands lying behind the horns. The gestation period is around 25 weeks, with a single kid born at dawn.

140

European Distribution

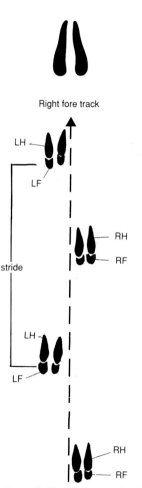

Right fore track

LH
LF

stride

RH
RF

LH
LF

RH
RF

Trotting gait with partial over-registration

amois (Order *Artiodactyla*)

nilar species: The Alpine Ibex (*Capra ibex*, page 138), Mouflon (*Ovis musimon*, page 136) and mestic goats cause confusion.

eld signs and clues: The almost spherical 1.5cm (0.6in) diameter droppings are the most frequent sign nearby Chamois. Since Chamois inhabit rocky terrain, their tracks are only obvious in snow and easure 6.5 x 4cm (2.6 x 1.6in). The cleaves are long and narrow, with a definite space between the two, since they are so manoeuvrable, the impressions can be variable. Both the toe and sole are deeply pressed, but the dew claws only show in snow and soft ground or when the Chamois moves rapidly. e lower part of the leg and foot are very flexible so that when the animal is frightened and bolts away, e legs bend, bringing the dew claws into contact with the ground, leaving impressions 10cm (4in) hind the heel of the cleaves. During a walk, the parallel tracks show almost perfect registration between e and hind feet, with a stride of 40–70cm (16–28in). This extends to 150cm (60in) during a gallop, en the tracks form distinct groups of 4 with the splayed cleaves pointing outwards.

Red Deer hind with calf

RED DEER *Body length:* **165–260cm** (65–102in). *Tail length:* **12–15cm** (4.7–5.9in).

Apart from the Elk, *Cervus elaphus* is the largest deer in Europe with a reddish-brown coat in summer and grey-brown in winter, when it becomes much thicker. From August to October the rut occurs and stags develop a shaggy mane which remains throughout the winter. Stags grow antlers from spring onwards, stripping the velvet in August and shedding them the following March. Flat blades are never formed, but mature stags have at least 10 points on their antlers which are interlocked during battles for the harem. A single calf is born May or June and is spotted for the first 8 weeks.

This species originated from deciduous forests, but is adaptable and now colonizes a variety of habitats, including moorland, mountain slopes and grassy plains, where they browse grass, leaves, buds and shoots. They are found in central and eastern Europe, but not in Scandinavia or Iceland. In the British Isles, native populations thrive in Scotland, north-west England and south-west Ireland, with feral herds elsewhere. The most familiar roaring and moaning bellows of the stags are heard during the autumn.

Similar species: The Sika Deer *(Cervus nippon*, page 144), Fallow Deer *(Cervus dama*, page 148) and Roe Deer *(Capreolus capreolus*, page 154) are likely to cause some confusion at a distance.

Field signs and clues: Red Deer leave numerous signs around the countryside, including shed antlers, frequently found individually rather than in pairs. In late summer males thrash their antlers against the branches and trunks of flexible saplings to remove the covering of soft skin or velvet. They usually eat the velvet, so it is rarely found, but the constant rubbing against the young trees causes them to fray, with the young bark torn off into characteristic long strips and many upper

142

Red Deer (Order *Artiodactyla*)

branches snapped off. A similar sign occurs during the rutting season, when the antlers are repeatedly struck against larger trees and leave plough marks in the bark and even torn strips.

   Red Deer enjoy wallowing in deep, swampy depressions along lake and river banks. Both sexes enjoy taking mud-baths and the well-trodden water-filled hollows are easy to find. Similar courtship wallows, made in soft mud by the antlers and forefeet, can be found during September and October. They fill with rain water and are then added to by the stag's urine, so that they are often located by smell alone. In spring and winter this species damages trees, especially young conifers, by browsing the new buds and shoots and stripping off bark 2–3m (6.56–9.8ft) from the ground.

   The tracks of this species are large, 8 x 7cm (3.1 x 2.75), and wider at the front in a distinct splay. The cleaves are rounded at both ends, but especially at the heel, and the dew claws only show in very soft ground. Cleaves are typically parallel to each other with convex outer margins. When Red Deer are walking, the hind feet tracks almost register perfectly into the forefoot tracks, with a stride of between 80–150cm (32–60in). During a trot the tracks do not register, but are arranged heel-to-toe, in a virtually straight line, whereas in bounding or jumping, all four tracks are placed in a tight group with the cleaves well splayed and dew claws often showing. There is 2–3m (6.5–9.8ft) between each group.

   The black or brown 2.5cm (1in) long acorn-shaped droppings are deposited in small groups. When alarmed the hind gives a gruff, hoarse bark and the calf a shrill scream.

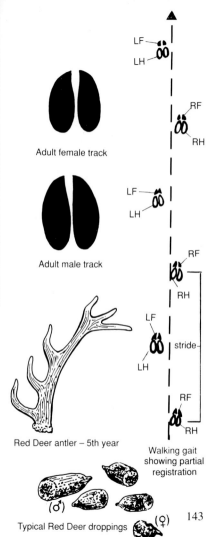

Adult female track

Adult male track

Red Deer antler – 5th year

Walking gait showing partial registration

(♂)

Typical Red Deer droppings (♀)

143

Sika Deer breed in feral herds

British Distribution

SIKA DEER *Body length:* **115–130cm** (45–51in). *Tail length:* **15cm** (5.9in).

Cervus nippon resembles a scaled-down Red Deer, with a reddish-brown summer coat liberally marked with creamy-white spots. During winter these spots fade and the coat turns dark grey-brown. The rump and tail are characteristic: the rump is white with dark edges, as in Fallow Deer, but the short tail is white without black markings. When alarmed, Sika erect their white rump hairs, making the patch very noticeable and providing a warning to the herd. The buck's antlers are similar to those of Red Deer, but bear only 8 points when fully grown.

Introduced into Britain about 120 years ago from eastern Asia, feral herds are widespread and in some areas they interbreed with Red Deer. Sika occur as feral herds throughout western Europe. Living in mixed woodland and scrubland, they are most active at dusk and dawn, when they graze. The rut occurs from September to November, during which the bucks emit a loud whistle, interspersed with typical roars. White-spotted calves are born during May and June.

144

European Distribution

Sika Deer (Order *Artiodactyla*)

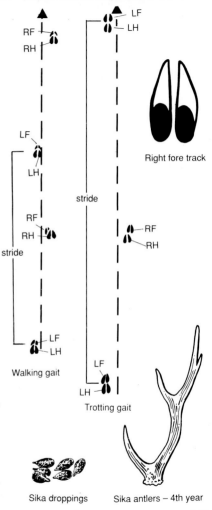

RF
RH

LF
LH

Right fore track

stride

LF
LH

stride

RF
RH

LF
LH

RF
RH

Walking gait

LF
LH

Trotting gait

Sika droppings

Sika antlers – 4th year

Similar species: The Red Deer (*Cervus elaphus*, page 142), Fallow Deer (*Cervus dama*, page 148) and Spotted Deer (*Cervus axis,* page 150) are all similar and misleading from a distance.

Field signs and clues: Wherever this deer is common, the antlers, which are shed in April, may be found. The black, currant-like droppings are often deposited in regular latrines, although they do occur randomly like those of other deer species. As with most deer, this species strips bark from trees and eats developing shoots and branches in springtime, causing some damage to commercial plantations.

Adults utter screaming alarm calls whenever they are disturbed, before running away. The tracks vary considerably according to sex and age, but in an adult stag measure up to 8 x 5cm (3.14 x 1.96 in). The cleaves are broad with rounded heels and pointed tips which splay in soft ground. Dew claw impressions show only when the deer slips in the mud. During a walking gait, fore and hind foot registration is almost perfect with a 100cm (39in) stride. Registration does not occur in the trotting gait, when the tracks appear heel-to-toe and in pairs.

145

Bull Elk with radio transmitter collar

No British Distribution

British Distribution

ELK *Body length:* Up to **290cm** (114in). *Tail length:* **4–5cm** (1.57–2in).

Alces alces is called the Moose in North America and Canada, but it is one of Europe's largest land mammals. They are easily recognized by their shaggy blackish-brown fur and long legs covered in grey-white fur. The antlers are huge and are generally flattened into broad shovel-like blades with numerous points. Others are less developed, with branching points but no flattened blades. Colonizing northern coniferous and deciduous forests or tundra, the Elk feeds on low-growing shrubs, shoots, tree bark and water plants. They often wade deep into lakes to uproot aquatic vegetation. Elks are generally solitary, but are both nocturnally and diurnally active, wandering miles in search of food. During September and October the rut begins and the forests echo to the roars, grunts and bellows of the bulls calling for a mate. Each bull mates with several cows, who give birth to 2–3 calves during May and June. They are suckled for about 10 months and can live for up to 25 years, since their only natural predator is the wolf, which has declined throughout Europe.

Similar species: Cannot really be confused with any other animal, but the Reindeer (*Rangifer tarandus*, page 152) is similar, although much slighter in build.

Field signs and clues: Because of the Elk's size any woodland path which is regularly used is cleared of overhanging vegetation up to a height of 250cm (98in) and 100cm (40in) wide. These well-cleared pathways are instantly recognizable. In winter they browse bark and new growing

146

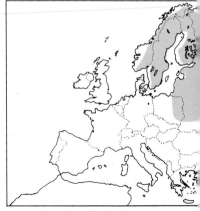
European Distribution

Elk or Moose (Order *Artiodactyla*)

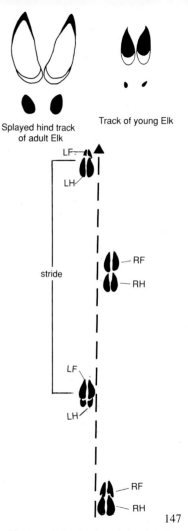

Splayed hind track
of adult Elk

Track of young Elk

stride

LF
LH

RF
RH

LF
LH

RF
RH

147

Trotting gait showing imperfect registration

shoots, regularly breaking off branches in the process by treading on the tree. These feeding signs are diagnostic and the large 2.5–5cm (1–1.96in) droppings are equally recognizable. They are generally pointed at one end and flattened, or slightly rounded at the other.

Elks may be heard uttering a muffled coughing, warning sound if wolves are nearby. Males and females communicate with each other by a series of soft guttural calls, especially during their courtship. Rutting wallows may be found where the males have excavated pits in soft mud with their forelegs and allowed them to fill with water before adding urine. They are usually discovered by their foul smells. Elk tracks are enormous, measuring 16.5 x 13cm (6.5 x 5.1in) and the cleaves with their pointed tips impress deeply. Dew claws are equally large and show well in soft mud. Elks usually walk or trot, and during a walk the hind and forefeet tracks partially register, producing a stride of 90–100cm (36–40in) in adults. Registration becomes imperfect or totally absent during a trot, when the stride increases to around 150cm (60in).

Fallow Deer fawn

British Distribution

FALLOW DEER *Body length:* **150–160cm** (59–63in). *Tail length:* **16–19cm** (6.2–7.4in).

Cervus dama is a variably coloured deer, but the majority show a reddish-brown ground colour with white spots in summer, turning to darker grey in winter. The tail and rump are diagnostic, since the rump is white with black margins and the tail, which constantly swings, has a bold black stripe down the dorsal side. Some individuals are pale grey-white or grey-black and lack all spots.

From April to June bucks shed their distinctive palmate antlers, which rapidly grow again and are stripped of their velvet in August ready for the autumn rut. Dominant bucks herd groups of does together and fiercely defend their harems, sparring with rival males and clashing their antlers together. The belching, muffled barks of the rutting bucks are familiar sounds across open woodland during October and November. Single fawns are born in June.

Originally native to Mediterranean woodlands, Fallow Deer have been introduced throughout Europe and were brought to Britain by the Normans, since when they have become popular in deer parks.

Similar species: The Red Deer (*Cervus elaphus*, page 142), Sika Deer (*Cervus nippon*, page 144) and Spotted Deer (*Cervus axis*, page 150).

Field signs and clues: The shed antlers of Fallow Deer are the most commonly found. During the mating season the bucks damage small trees by fraying them with their antlers. They also mark

148

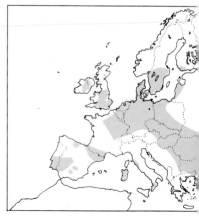

European Distribution

Fallow Deer (Order *Artiodactyla*)

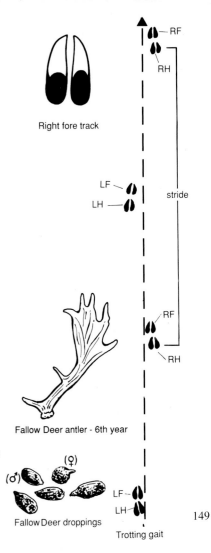

Right fore track

stride

Fallow Deer antler - 6th year

(♂) (♀)
Fallow Deer droppings

Trotting gait

the boundaries of their territories with a musky scent, which can be detected by the human nose. Fallow Deer are notorious for barking trees, and damaged trunks are a good indication of their presence. The droppings are black, shiny and cylindrical. They are pointed at one end when deposited by a male deer and measure 1.5cm (0.6in) long. Female deer deposit droppings with rounded ends and although they occur in latrine piles during the summer, they are randomly scattered in winter.

The tracks made by the doe measure about 5.5 x 3.5cm (2.16 x 1.37in), whereas those of the buck are 8 x 5cm (3.14 x 1.96in). They are characterized by the almost straight outer margins at the rear of the cleaves. Two small dew claws only show behind the main cleaves in very soft ground, and splaying is unusual. Whenever walking, the Fallow Deer produces a trail with virtually perfect registration between fore and hind feet, with a stride of 60cm (24in). During a trot the tracks do not register so perfectly and the heel-to-toe trail results. At full gallop, when the deer escapes from danger, all four tracks are grouped together with a stride of about 110cm (44in) between groups.

149

Spotted or Axis Deer

SPOTTED DEER or AXIS DEER *Body length:* up to **130cm** (51 in).

   Slightly smaller than the familiar Fallow Deer, *Cervus axis* has a reddish-brown coat covered in white spots, which remain throughout the year. The tail is long and covers a white rump without the black markings, found on the similarly marked Fallow Deer. A white throat patch is clearly visible. Unlike the Fallow Deer, which has broad-bladed antlers, those of the Spotted Deer are long and slender with a maximum of 3 points each side when fully developed.

   Originally from India and Sri Lanka, the Spotted Deer was introduced to zoos and reserves in Europe, and has become established in the wild, as in Istria, Yugoslavia. It is typically a woodland species, and the harsh, bellowing, rutting call of the bucks is often heard echoing through the glades of woods in Italy and northern Yugoslavia. During autumn the deer feeds on wild fruits, browsing leaves and shoots at other times of the year. This species is gregarious and diurnally active.

European Distribution

150

Spotted Deer (Order *Artiodactyla*)

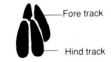

Right fore track

Right hind track

Track showing slipping of cleaves
common to this species.

Fore track

Hind track

Tracks showing partial registration
common during the walking gait

Similar species: The Red Deer (*Cervus elaphus*, page 142), Sika Deer (*Cervus nippon*, page 144) and Fallow Deer (*Cervus dama*, page 148).
Field signs and clues: During autumn this species is particularly fond of eating wild hedgerow and tree fruits. Once such feeding localities have been discovered, observing the deer is possible by keeping downwind of them and remaining quiet and concealed. Although there is no fixed rutting season, the stags are highly vocal during the mating period. The challenge call of the stag is a haunting, wild scream, repeated several times. If the hind is frightened, they utter a hare-like scream.

A medium-size track is characterized by its asymmetrical, tapering cleaves, which have slightly convex outer walls. There is limited splay and the dew claws do not show. During the walking gait, the fore and hind feet tracks are partially registered with a stride of 60cm (24in), but as the pace increases to a trot, the trail shows paired heel-to-toe tracks with a stride of 90cm (36in).

151

Reindeer in Cairngorms

REINDEER *Body length:* up to **220cm** (86.6in). *Tail length:* **10–15cm** (4–6in).

    Rangifer tarandus is the only species of deer where both sexes grow antlers, although those of the male are larger. Cows carry their antlers until the spring, whereas the bulls drop their antlers in autumn. Reindeer are variable in colour, but their summer coat is generally grey-brown with the winter coat a lighter grey. A mountain race and a separate forest race originally occurred in northern Europe. These have slowly been replaced by domesticated reindeer. Isolated colonies of Mountain Reindeer remain in Norway, while Forest Reindeer are still found in Russia and Finland, so that in the wild, Arctic tundra, taiga and open woodland are the main habitats. Two hundred thousand years ago reindeer roamed Britain, but became extinct, and were only re-introduced in 1952 to roam the Cairngorms near Aviemore.

Similar species: The Red Deer (*Cervus elaphus*, page 142), Elk (*Alces alces*, page 146) and Fallow Deer (*Cervus dama*, page 148) all cause confusion.

Field signs and clues: Reindeer do not cause tree damage by browsing, but feed almost exclusively on lichen, especially a species called Reindeer Moss (*Cladonia rangiferina*). They can even locate their food under snow by digging down with their front legs, and these excavations are a positive sign of a Reindeer herd feeding nearby. Their bottle-shaped droppings are variable, from 1.5–2.5cm (0.6–1in) in diameter and deposited randomly. In winter they are black or green-brown, but become yellow-brown in the summer and are easily recognized. The

152

British Distribution

European Distribution

Reindeer (Order *Artiodactyla*)

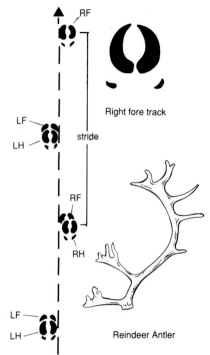

Right fore track

Reindeer Antler

Walking gait showing almost perfect registration

large, broad track is quickly identifiable because of the two half-moon shaped cleaves, forming an almost circular impression 9cm (3.6in) long and 10cm (4in) wide with a large gap in the middle. The cleaves frequently splay and the large dew claws which are set low down on the foot always show, even when the reindeer is walking slowly on firm ground. The track of the cows is slightly smaller and more pointed than those made by bulls.

This species generally walks or trots through its habitat and during the walking gait the fore and hind foot tracks show almost perfect registration, with an average stride of 40cm (16in). Whenever trotting, the tracks turn slightly outwards, do not register perfectly; and the stride decreases.

Reindeer Droppings

Roe buck – early morning

British Distribution

ROE DEER *Body length:* up to **135cm** (53in).

Capreolus capreolus is Britain's smallest indigenous deer, with a red-brown coat and buff rump in summer, changing to grey-brown during September–October with a white rump. Bucks have short antlers, with a maximum of 3 points, which are roughened around their base. They are fully developed in May, when the velvet is rubbed off, and are shed in early winter. Fawns born during May and June are dark brown with rows of white spots along their back and flanks, which disappear after 2 months.

Found throughout most of Europe, Roe Deer inhabit woodlands and adjacent fields, where they browse trees and shrubs, especially bramble. In the British Isles they are absent from Ireland, Wales and parts of central England, whereas in Scotland, where they are most common, they are seen on open moorland. Highly territorial throughout the year, bucks aggressively defend their territory from May and during the rut, which begins in July. Both sexes bark, but does also produce a disyllabic whistle during the mating season.

Similar species: Although there is a difference in size, the Muntjac (*Muntiacus reevesi,* page 156) and Chinese Water Deer (*Hydropotes inermis,* page 158) cause confusion.

Field signs and clues: Roe Deer cause some visible damage to trees by eating new growing shoots and stripping bark up to a height of 100cm (39.37in), especially young conifers. They also fray small trees with their antlers and create characteristic, worn pathways around a specific tree

154

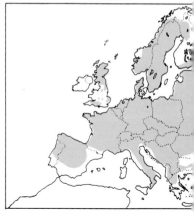

European Distribution

Roe Deer (Order *Artiodactyla*)

or bush. The significance of this behaviour is unknown, but the circular paths are easy to find, particularly during July and August. Males mark their territory by rubbing head scent glands against vegetation and leaving a musty odour. They also mark territorial boundaries by churning up the ground with their forefeet. The black or dark brown droppings measure 1.5–2cm (0.6–0.78in) and are similar to those of sheep, goats or Brown Hare. They are pointed at one end and flattened at the other, and although regular latrines are used near the deer's feeding grounds, they are also randomly scattered along the trail.

Tracks are characteristic because of the narrow, sharply pointed cleaves making an impression 5 x 4cm (1.96 x 1.57in). The outer walls of each cleave are strongly convex and in soft ground the track is obviously heart-shaped. In soft ground, the dew claws show well and there is noticeable splaying of the cleaves. During a walk, the hind foot registers imperfectly with the forefoot track, and a stride of 40–60cm (16–24in). As speed increases to a trot the tracks do not register, but are positioned heel-to-toe in a virtual straight line. During a gallop the tracks are placed in groups of 4 with 2–3m (6.5–9.8ft) between groups.

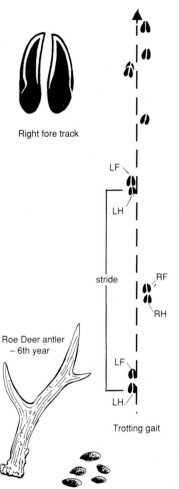

Right fore track

stride

LF
LH

RF
RH

LF

LH

Trotting gait

Roe Deer antler
– 6th year

Roe Deer droppings

155

Muntjac or Barking Deer

British Distribution

MUNTJAC *Body length:* up to **90cm** (35in).

Similar in size to a fox, *Muntiacus reevesi* has a glossy red-brown summer coat with a white rump which is only noticeable when the deer lifts its tail when alarmed. Bucks have short, backwardly curved antlers bearing two points which are shed May and June, but reach full size again during October and November. The upper canines of the bucks are elongated, forming tusks which protrude from the lips, and during territorial fights they are used as weapons, rather than the antlers.

Introduced into Britain from China in 1900, many escaped from their private estates and are now well established in southern England, where they colonize woodland and dense scrubland. There is no specific mating season and since does are able to conceive within a few days of fawning they can fawn every 7 months. Successful breeding is causing an extension of their range. Active by day or night Muntjac are mostly seen at dusk, browsing shrubs, trees and eating fruits. Muntjac utter loud barks over prolonged periods and equally loud distress calls.

Similar species: The Roe Deer (*Capreolus capreolus*, page 154) and Chinese Water Deer (*Hydropotes inermis*, page 158) are similar, although they vary in size.

Field signs and clues: Since the Muntjac uses regular routes and feeding areas, one positive sign is the well-worn pathway or 'tunnel' through low-growing vegetation. Saplings on the edge of these paths become well worn by body friction and a distinct musky odour can be detected on the

156

No European Distribution

European Distribution

Muntjac (Order *Artiodactyla*)

Right fore track

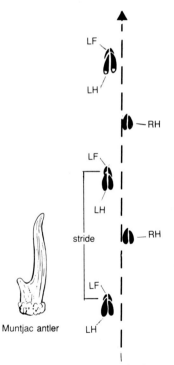

foliage. This scent is deposited by the males, particularly during the breeding season, October to March. Occasionally it is possible to find browsing evidence of Muntjac, because they do strip some bark from small trees and chew developing shoots. Their cylindrical droppings are small black or dark brown pellets about 1cm (0.4in) long, and are similar to those of sheep or goats. They are deposited in regular latrines around the feeding area, but also randomly along their trails.

    Muntjac tracks are instantly recognized because the cleaves are distorted and of uneven size. They are often less than 3cm (1.18in) long, pointed at the toe and narrow. Since the dew claws are small they generally only leave a mark in soft ground or when the animal is jumping, which also causes the cleaves to splay. When the deer is walking the hind feet tracks almost register perfectly with the forefeet tracks, producing a stride of 25–30cm (10–12in). The registration becomes less perfect as the deer begins to trot, and as it gallops the tracks are arranged in groups of 4 with a stride of over 1m (3.28ft) between the groups.

Muntjac antler

Walking gait showing 157
near perfect registration

Chinese Water Deer are feral escapees

CHINESE WATER DEER *Body length:* up to **100cm** (39in).

Ranging in size between the Muntjac and Roe Deer, *Hydropotes inermis* is the only deer found in Europe without antlers. In summer the coat is reddish-brown, paling to a denser, paler grey-brown pelage in winter. The large, rounded ears, black eyes and nose are highly characteristic, as are the buck's protruding tusk-like canine teeth in the upper jaw.

Originating from the damp valleys of north-east China, it was introduced to Woburn Park in Bedfordshire, England, earlier this century. Escapees have formed feral populations in the Cambridgeshire Fens and East Anglian Broads amongst the reed beds and alder scrubland. Feral herds also occur in France. They are generally nocturnal and solitary creatures, grazing root crops and grass, but uttering screams whenever disturbed. During November–December the rut occurs with constant barking, squealing and whickering as they chase each other. The fawns are born during May and June and may number as many as 6, but twins are most common.

British Distribution

No European Distribution

European Distribution

158

Right fore track showing dew claws

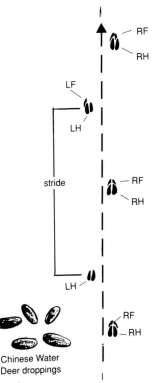

Walking gait showing near perfect registration

Chinese Water Deer droppings

inese Water Deer (Order *Artiodactyla*)

milar species: The Roe Deer (*Capreolus capreolus*, page 154) and Muntjac (*Muntiacus reevesi*, page 6) are similar in appearance but vary in size.

eld signs and clues: One of the characteristic signs of this species are the narrow pathways which are servable in reed beds and dense vegetation surrounding marshland. A strong musty odour occurs along ese routes and the scent is deposited by males marking their territories. The small, cigar-shaped, black oppings measure 1.5 x 0.5cm (0.6 x 0.2in) and are deposited in small piles along the deer's pathways.

    Their tracks are distinctive because they are long and narrow, measuring 5 x 3cm (1.96 x 1.18in), with inted cleaves. Whereas the gap between the cleaves is wide, the diagnostic feature is the flat inner edge the hooves. At speed, the small dew claws show up in the track and often their cleaves splay.

    This species most often walks through its habitat and the tracks of the hind and forefeet show almost rfect registration, with a stride of 30–40cm (11.8–16in). As speed increases to a trot the registration of e tracks breaks down with the straight heel-to-toe trail characteristic of many dew species. During a llop, all 4 tracks are grouped together, with the dew claws clearly noticeable. A distance of about 1m 28ft) separates each group of tracks.

Species Index

References in **bold** are the main pages where the mammal is described, together with colour photographs. Other references indicate where the species is mentioned in the text.